TEMPTING FATE

By

BOB RAHN

WITH ROSARIO RAUSA

SPECIALTY PRESS

ISBN: 0-933424-81-7

Library of Congress Catalog Card No.: 95-72890

Text by Robert Rahn with Rosario "Zip" Rausa

Edited by: John W. Lambert

Published by:
      Specialty Press Publishers and Wholesalers
      11481 Kost Dam Road
      North Branch, MN 55056
      Phone: 800-895-4585

Book Trade Distribution by:
      Voyageur Press
      123 North Second Street
      Stillwater, MN 55082
      Phone: 800-888-9653
      Fax: 612-430-2211

PREFACE

(Edward H. Heinemann, the great aircraft designer—known as Mr. Attack Aviation as well as the Genius of El Segundo—passed away on November 26, 1991 at the age of 83. He outlined this foreword in early 1991 for inclusion in Bob Rahn's autobiography. It has been slightly edited by the authors.)

Bob Rahn was one of the most skilled and reliable test pilots in the aviation industry and especially at the Douglas Aircraft Company. He came to us at Douglas after combat and test flying duty with the Army Air Force and participated in the development of the "Sky" series of tactical aircraft for the U.S. Navy and Marine Corps during a remarkably productive period for Douglas from the late 1940s to the early 1960s.

Bob was perfectly equipped to be an experimental test pilot. Not only was he a solid, experienced aviator, he approached the job with true professionalism, thoroughly studying each aircraft before he flew it and working intimately and effectively with the ground support team of engineers and technicians. He respected them as they did him. Together, they forged a team with a common goal: producing the best possible aircraft for the prospective buyer.

Experimental test flying was and remains serious business with high stakes. Simply put, in those days at Douglas, if an airplane didn't meet the performance requirements, we wouldn't get a contract. And the Navy had stringent requirements indeed. Its airplanes had to withstand not only high g flight but the incredible rigors of carrier operations on the high seas. It was up to Bob, his fellow test pilots, and the indispensable support group to satisfy those requirements.

Bob earned a reputation for being extremely cool under the most "heated" circumstances. This will come through in his autobiography. He does not over dramatize the various emergencies he encountered over his long career but describes them in a matter of fact manner, because that's the way he was. Perhaps this cool, matter of fact demeanor accounts for his remarkable success as a test pilot.

We were going higher and faster at an unprecedented rate during this heyday at Douglas and Bob Rahn played a key role in the quantum jump in aviation technology we all achieved.

Amazingly, Bob transitioned from piston-powered aircraft to jet machines without a blink. He excelled. He was a natural. Most important to me as the Chief Engineer, however, was Bob's pure flying ability. Even when the aircraft gave him trouble, he brought 'em back.

Ed Heinemann
Rancho Santa Fe, California

INTRODUCTION

Chuck Yeager and I were sitting at the Edwards Air Force Base Officer's Club bar late one afternoon following a day of flight testing in the California skies in the early 1950s. I was a civilian test pilot for the Douglas Aircraft Company and Chuck was an Air Force Major similarly engaged with the Air Force. Our professional flying trails had crossed many times.

In the course of the conversation at the bar Chuck said, "Bob, you civilian test pilots are not qualified for test flying."

That immediately got my back up. I replied, "What the hell do you mean, we're not qualified? Ninety percent of us have a military background and are graduates of a military test pilot school. (The other 10 percent are flight testing commercial aircraft.) We've flown combat. That's why we were hired—because we had as much, or more experience than the average military test pilot. I resent that remark and don't agree with you!"

I had earned my civilian private pilot license in 1939 and joined the Army Air Corps in May 1941. Chuck began pilot training in early 1942. I had served a tour of combat flying Spitfires in the European and Mediterranean Theaters in 1942-1943 while Chuck flew P-51s in the European Theater in 1944-1945. I shot down my first enemy aircraft in 1943. He scored his first victory in 1944. I had done test work as an Army Air Force pilot in 1943 for the first time at Muroc, California and Chuck was there for the first time in 1945. He flew P-39s at Tonopah, Nevada (home of today's F-117 Stealth planes) in 1943 and I had conducted guided bomb testing at the same bases in 1944. I had also flown P-39s in 1942 in the 31st Fighter Group while in New Orleans.

I flew my first jet, the P-59, in 1944. Chuck flew it in 1945. I was in the second class of the Air Force Test Pilot School in early 1945 and Yeager was in the Class of 1946. We both had wheels-up crash landings in prop aircraft in a field while assigned to Wright Field. He hit a farm house and came out unscathed while I managed to avoid one, but bouncing around among the trees I also came out unhurt. Yeager did have one experience that I never had and that was to fly a rocket plane. Chuck left Edwards AFB and testing in 1954 and I stopped full time flight testing in 1957. I helped bring the 31st Fighter Group up to strength in 1942, and he joined the same Group in 1959.

So, in many key respects, our careers ran in parallel. I spoke with confidence, therefore, when the conversation in the bar at Edwards in the 1950s turned to the issue of military versus civilian test pilots.

Chuck was persuasive when he said, "The problem is you guys fly only one airplane for two, three, or maybe more years. Your knowledge is limited. You can't compare one aircraft's performance, stability and control characteristics over another. You don't know what other contractors are doing and what designs are good."

In the days that followed I gave this a lot of thought. Anger and resentment gave grudgingly away to reason. Chuck had a point and I decided to take advantage of it. I approached my management in the Douglas company and suggested that it might be a good idea if I could fly other "competing" aircraft, for the purpose Chuck cited. I was pleased as punch when they agreed. They sent a letter to the appropriate officials in the Navy and the Air Force and that led to my flying a variety of other aircraft in both services, including nearly the entire "Century" series of Air Force fighters— the first civilian, I believe, to do so.

Having the exposure to other planes, I am convinced, made me a more effective test pilot, and I am thankful to Chuck Yeager for starting that argument with me over two generations ago.

ACKNOWLEDGMENTS

The following people were of immense help to me in writing this book. Their assistance is deeply appreciated: R.B. Smith, Jay Reutz, K.E. Van Every, John Barter, Mal Abzug, Gunnar Anderson, Harry Gann, George Jansen, Jack Armstrong, John Brizendine, Donald Douglas Jr., Mel Oleson, Jim Stegman, Herman Knickerbocker, Steve Tydeman, Bob Brush, Jerry Pearson, B.J. Long, George Lehman, Phil Wiltsie, Marvin Miles, Nick Williams and Ed Heinemann.

PROLOGUE
Brigadier General Chuck Yeager, USAF (Ret.)

Bob Rahn and I are among the lucky ones. We helped introduce the world to the jet age, and in the process, we had the exciting, if not occasionally precarious, privilege of wringing out flying machines that doubled, even tripled the performance of their piston-powered predecessors.

The best test pilots possess first-rate mental and motor skills, love to fly, and share an unrelenting curiosity about the aircraft they are assigned to test. They must know the ins and outs of their bird, and be ready to handle it when it misbehaves. Bob Rahn possessed these characteristics in spades and applied them to his work, primarily for the Douglas Aircraft Company at a time when that organization was turning out an amazing string of successful combat aircraft, mostly for the U.S. Navy.

Like most test pilots, Bob encountered a fair share of emergencies. I was on his wing the day his F4D Skyray unexpectedly pitched violently upward, overstressing the aircraft and wrinkling its entire skin. Bob blacked out, revived as the fighter was plunging straight down toward the Pacific Ocean and with only a few thousand feet of altitude to play with, managed to pull out. Wisely, he aimed directly toward the nearest airfield, which happened to be Los Angeles International Airport, nursed the crippled Skyray down to a smooth landing and saved himself and the airplane.

It is testimony to Bob's skill under pressure that he succeeded in this instance. It is also noteworthy that Bob refers often in his autobiography to a mysterious companion in the cockpit: Fate. When the technicians examined the wrinkled Skyray, they found that the engine had torn loose from its mounts. A rough turn here or there and a bad situation could have gotten worse in a hurry.

Bob Rahn respects fate, or luck, or destiny—whatever you want to call it—as do I. It is a vital part of this enlightening and entertaining account of his eventful life in aviation, a life that extends from Spitfires in the European Theater of Operations with the Army Air Force in WW II, through civilian test pilot duty in the famed "Sky" series of Douglas aircraft (Skyraider, Skyknight, Skywarrior, Skyhawk, Skyray, and Skylancer), and on into America's space program.

Although I was an Air Force pilot and Bob was, primarily, a civilian aviator, our goals as experimental test pilots were the same: to help produce the best possible aircraft for the United States. With flyers like Bob Rahn at the controls, we couldn't help but succeed in that endeavor.

Bob Rahn was a cut above most of the other civilian test pilots I knew. He was that good!

DEDICATION

Every aviator has a collection of memorabilia that is special to him or her. I'm no exception. A glass tabletop on the outside deck of our home in Whittier, California, is a side cockpit window which I discovered in the trash can one day at the Douglas plant. It had been installed in an experimental aircraft, the X-3, but was taken out because it had a slight deformity. I got permission to take it home, converted it into a cocktail table and have enjoyed it ever since.

I have a section of skin, with a swastika on it, from a German JU88 medium bomber, downed in North Africa. I possess a silk scarf from an old parachute that my primary cadet classmates signed in 1941. It is so fragile now that when I touch it, it almost turns to dust.

I have the drag chute which helped me recover from a flat spin in the AD-3W Skyraider and cherish it as an item which has contributed to my longevity. I also have the ski pole which I managed to stick above my head as I was deluged by snow during an avalanche. It was my lifeline to survival.

Most importantly, I have the memory of working with a legion of experts who were a major part of my professional life and helped me through countless travails and accomplishments in the sky. The bond I feel toward them can never be broken.

Therefore, I dedicate this book to all the flight test engineers, design engineers, and aircraft technicians whose skill, ingenuity and determination were with me on every test flight I made.

I know little of military aviation, and even less of experimental flying, which is perhaps the most inspiring and yet fateful of all. These divisions deserve their own written testimony.

Fate is the Hunter
By Ernest K. Gann

1

EARLY YEARS

I flew out over the Pacific leaving the California coastline behind me and positioned myself for the dive. At 12,000 feet, with the sky all around me clear of clouds and airborne traffic, I pushed over, checked the attitude gyro to ensure I had achieved the required 90-degree dive angle, and as the altimeter needle swept through 8,000 feet, holding the XBT2D as steady as possible, I pressed the bomb pickle. I heard and felt a distinct thud, indicating that the inert bomb had left the aircraft.

Four seconds later, still in the dive, all hell broke loose. The bomb had struck the propeller, apparently ripping off one of the four blades. Suddenly, it was as if the XBT2D had gone into convulsions. It was totally out of sync and undergoing a severe anti-symmetric load condition. There was an indescribably terrible noise and a shaking in front of me for a second or two, so severe I couldn't even read my instruments. Next thing I knew, the engine had torn away from its mounts.

Everything was suddenly very quiet. The aircraft began a crazy tumble in the sky, with me in it. I had entered the scary regime of uncontrolled flight.

With the propeller and the engine gone, the center of gravity (CG) had abruptly shifted aft. The aircraft was buffeting and toppling over as it fell wildly toward earth. I couldn't get hold of the hand mike to notify flight operations at El Segundo that I was in trouble and had to bail out.

I opened the canopy and reached for the safety belt handle. The instant it released, my body popped out of the airplane as if I were a ping-pong ball flung into the breeze. Pulling the ripcord, I got a good chute and from about 5,000 feet, began the descent toward the water. I caught a glimpse of the stricken XBT2D. How strange it looked without an engine and propeller, flopping downward like a shotgunned duck.

In the descent I had time to contemplate the water landing. I had read about pilots landing in the sea during the war only to drown from becoming entangled in the canopy and shroud lines. I released my leg straps and just prior to entry into the waves, unhooked the chest strap. When I hit, I purposely stayed under the surface as long as possible allowing the wind to blow the canopy away from me, then rose safely to the surface.

It was late afternoon and I was eight miles offshore from El Segundo. I knew it would be some time before the company realized I had had an emergency. Help might be a long time coming.

Well, I asked for it. I left the Air Force to become an experimental test pilot for the Douglas Aircraft Company. I should have known there would be days like this.

My aviation career really began when Charles Lindbergh came to Dayton, Ohio one day in the fall of 1927 and changed my life forever. I was seven years old then, and he was aviation's hero of heroes. Alone, he had made a historic crossing of the Atlantic in the "Spirit of St. Louis." Now, he was touring the U.S. in the same single-engine airplane that had carried him on that unforgettable journey.

All eyes were trained toward the sky when he lumbered toward the city. I was in the backyard of our home when I saw the Spirit approaching. As luck would have it, Lindbergh flew directly over our house in his descent toward the destination airstrip. I was awestruck as his airplane roared past. Something happened inside me. I couldn't explain it, but I was overwhelmed and so exhilarated by the experience that I vowed, then and there, that flying was for me. From that moment on, I was absolutely determined to become an aviator!

I was born in Harvey, Illinois, a suburb of Chicago, on December 29, 1920. Both my father, Rudolf John Rahn, and my mother, Ruth Ohrman Rahn, were graduates of the University of Illinois. Dad was a mechanical engineer, Mom, a teacher. We moved quite often in my early years. Dad had jobs in Connecticut and Washington D.C., as well as Ohio. Eventually, he founded the "Rahn Granite Surface Plate Company" of Dayton with my older brother, Ivan, who retired as Factory Manager. A younger brother, Don, was also an aviation enthusiast and flew fighters in the Air Force before joining the family surface plate business where he worked his way up to President of the company.

I had a wonderful youth with plenty of adventuresome friends. Yet I always dreamed of one day becoming a pilot. I had a paper route that earned me enough pennies to catch the Saturday afternoon serial featuring "Tailspin Tommy," the handsome and daring aviator who always saved the day. (Years later, I befriended "Tailspin Tommy" Brown. He had quit the silver screen to become a test pilot at Douglas Aircraft.)

As I neared high school graduation, with Dad's encouragement, I decided to pursue an aeronautical engineering degree.This would fit in nicely with my aspirations to fly. I took advantage of the University of Cincinnati's cooperative engineering program: study seven weeks, then work eight weeks, over a five-year period. I did OK with the books but couldn't get excited about the interim jobs, cleaning spittoons and machinery at the General Motors Delco Brake Company, or sharpening drill bits and attaching a spring to automobile brakes on the assembly line. The pay was $26 a week, but the labor was a far cry from aviation.

In my junior year I landed a job as a draftsman at Wright Field, which was closer to my goals, although it involved a pay cut down to $20 a week.

Then, in 1939, the government originated the Civilian Pilot Training Program, a godsend for me. President Roosevelt believed the U.S. might get involved in the war already underway in Europe and wanted to train as many pilots as possible, just in case.

College students, therefore, could get their pilot's license at no cost. I jumped at the opportunity, was soon learning to fly in a single-engine, high-wing Luscombe and qualified for my license in 1939 at the age of 18.

In addition to basic flight maneuvers we were taught intentional spins and spin recovery. For many students spins were exciting, terrifying and often disorienting. For me, for reasons I could not understand, they were routine acrobatic maneuvers. Executing the proper procedures and recovering from whirling spirals seemed second nature. Indeed, I enjoyed them but was unexcited by them. I had no idea this idiosyncrasy was of any special value. I suppose it was just a case of my being comfortable in the cockpit. Although I probably should have been, I was neither intimidated by the airplane nor the instructor. Later, as my flying career progressed, I came to realize that this ability to maintain a cool demeanor under stressful circumstances was a gift. I did nothing to earn it.

After one flight involving several spins, all of which I handled as taught, the instructor made a memorable entry in my log book. "The flight was satisfactory," he wrote, "but the student doesn't appear to be interested in flying." Apparently, I had not reacted in the animated manner expected of a neophyte.

(Incidentally, the log book containing the instructor's words is on display aboard the **USS Yorktown** Museum in Charleston, SC.)

Over a five month period in 1940 I logged six flights but only two hours and 40 minutes in the air. Between the time I got my license until May 1941, when I joined the Army Air Corps, I flew little due to the cost – six dollars an hour – a lot of money in those days. For more than monetary reasons, however, I treasured every moment in the sky.

In the meantime, I wasn't exactly lighting up the sky with my grades. Becoming a successful engineer was in doubt. In my heart of hearts I wanted to become an airline pilot and considered joining the Army Air Corps. With Uncle Sam's help, I could accumulate the necessary flight hours to qualify. Unfortunately, candidates had to be 20 years old, with two years of college in their background. I was only 19 so I had little choice but to put in another year at school.

When the time came I passed the Air Corps' physical exam, although it was nip and tuck with the eyes. I was accepted for aviation cadet training and ordered to report to Muskogee, Oklahoma, for primary flight training. My parents saw me off at the train station in Dayton. My mother's caution to me as I boarded the train remains vivid in my memory today, more than 50 years later.

"Son," she said, with the sincere urgency of mothers through the ages, "please fly low and slow!" My mother was no master of aerodynamics and certainly did not realize the hazards of flight in the low and slow regime. But her heart was in the right place and I have never forgotten her well-intentioned words that day at the train station.

In May 1941 I checked in for primary training at Muskogee, a small town on the banks of the Arkansas River about 50 miles southeast of Tulsa.

Written in huge letters across the wings of our blue and yellow PT-19 trainers on the flight line at the Air Corps base, was "U.S. ARMY." When I got into the sky, all alone on my first solo flight, after only six hours of instruction, I looked at those letters and shouted, "I'm an *Army* pilot now!" Which was premature, of course. Yet I couldn't help being overwhelmed with pride at this achievement, modest as it was.

I also could not believe that the Army was *paying* me $70 a month to learn how to fly. On top of that, they fed me and put a roof over my head. For a 20 year-old from Dayton, Ohio, acclimated to the drudgery of assembly-line work, this was an incredible experience.

After Oklahoma it was San Angelo, Texas, where we flew the BT-13. Its sizable radial engine produced 450 horsepower and constituted a noticeable step up from the 175 horsepower in-line power plant of the PT-19.

When we weren't studying or flying we prowled the local bars. I didn't drink in college, but as an aviation cadet I began to imbibe. Seems like all of us did. Rum and cokes were a favorite. San Angelo offered little in the way of excitement and there weren't many girls around. I suppose this had something to do with the inclination to tip a few.

Flying was our overriding concern, though, and we had to keep focused because the "wash-out" rate in pre-World War II days was almost 50 percent.

When asked if I wanted single-engine or twin-engine instruction I opted for the latter since my ultimate ambition was to become an airline pilot. Nonetheless, as it turned out then and subsequently, I was always assigned to single-engine training.

Advanced flight school was at Brooks Field in San Antonio, Texas, where the AT-6's 650 horsepower engine, retractable landing gear and mass of instruments for all-weather flying constituted yet another step up. One of our pastimes was to gather in front of the mess hall overlooking the runway to watch our fellow aviators ground loop the Curtiss O-52, another aircraft we flew after getting our wings. It was a little bit like searching the skies for shooting stars on a summer night. There weren't an awful lot of them, but when somebody did swirl around clumsily in his 0-52 on the ground, the spectacle was exhilarating and provided a lot of laughs.

One day we had a little more excitement than we cared for as one of the 0-52s settled onto the roof of the mess hall during take-off because the pilot pumped the flaps up too soon. We moved our observation site after that.

It was at Brooks Field, incidentally, that I earned a nickname which stayed with me for much of my Air Corps days. We played a lot of basketball when we weren't flying, and I had a tendency to bull my way toward the basket, incurring charging calls with considerable frequency. During one scrimmage a fellow cadet called me "Stormy," because of that tendency, and the sobriquet stuck.

Everybody of my generation remembers where they were on December 7, 1941, when the Japanese bombed Pearl Harbor. I was at a bowling alley with a date. Reports of the attack blared over the radio along with the order that all military personnel report to base immediately.

We rushed to Brooks Field and joined in the effort to disperse the aircraft as a precautionary measure should Japanese bombers find their way to Texas. We knew that was unlikely, of course, but there was great urgency in the air nonetheless, and the commanding officer of the base feared he might have been chastised absent some dramatic gesture.

I was in class 42A, the first class scheduled to graduate in 1942. The declaration of war accelerated the pace of training and we were winged on January 9th, several weeks earlier than planned. Since I lacked a special girl friend at the time, my parents pinned on my wings. The cut-off age for getting a commission was twenty-one, a deadline I met by eleven days, allowing me to wear the single gold bar of a second lieutenant.

My parents arrived in the 1940 Buick convertible I had purchased second-hand for $900. This was my first car, a cream colored beauty. Even though war was raging, I was on top of the world. I was a freshly minted aviator, had a few dollars in my pocket (I now got $240 per month as a flying officer) and a shiny convertible to scoot about.

About half of Class 42A was ordered to New Orleans in March 1942 to flesh out the roster of the 31st Fighter Group which consisted of the 307th, 308th and 309th squadrons. I was assigned to the 309th commanded by First Lieutenant Harry Thyng who was as aggressive as he was enthusiastic. Harry was only 24 years old but to me he was a seasoned veteran. At 21, I was a genuine rookie.

At an introductory meeting Harry told us that if we lived to acquire 1,000 hours in fighters, we probably would survive to fulfill a career as an aviator. With less than 300 hours, I was in the danger zone.

We checked out in the Curtiss P-40B Tomahawk, my first fighter. It had a long, in-line engine, a decisive change for those of us used to radial power plants. Contrary to my behavior when it came to spinning a trainer, my legs were shaking noticeably on the rudder pedals before taking off in the 1,200 horse power Tomahawk. The P-40 was considered a ground looper, but our training in the O-52 helped to alleviate this problem.

The Tomahawk had a big cockpit for a fighter and, because of its long nose, we had to "S" turn the airplane while taxiing to see where we were going. We had a man in our squadron nicknamed "Tiger" who just barely made the minimum height requirement. Every time he taxied by, people gave a double take because what they saw was a P-40 S-ing down the taxiway with *nobody* aboard. I managed to get the airplane up and down safely.

After a few hours in the P-40 we were assigned to the Bell P-39 Airacobra whose most noteworthy characteristic was its in-line engine mounted behind the pilot. It had tricycle landing gear (two main wheels and a nose wheel) and a 37- millimeter cannon which fired through the hub of the propeller. On my two attempts to fire it, the cannon jammed, an obvious frustration in combat. So much for reliability.

The Airacobra was fast and had excellent ground handling characteristics, but for dog fighting it left something to be desired. We lost several P-39s due to flat spins though test pilots from the manufacturer, Bell Aircraft, insisted they had never experienced the phenomenon.

One afternoon I was "tail-end Charlie" in a formation of four Airacobras returning to New Orleans after a cross-country fight. We had to vector around a number of thunderstorms which had towered up in our path. I had to use more power than the others, just to keep up. Also, we had guzzled a lot more fuel than planned because of the thunderstorms. I was on empty when I elected to make a precautionary landing in a grass field rather than chance flying over Lake Pontchartrain and risk losing the airplane.

I landed OK but toward the end of the roll-out I hit a rut and snapped off the nose gear. We didn't have a shoulder harness in those days, just lap belts. I jolted forward and hit my face on the instrument panel and gun sight, but without serious injury. This was my first crash in an airplane, but the P-39 had better days ahead, was repaired and returned to duty.

Since we were chosen to be the first fighter group in the European Theater of Operations (ETO), the legendary Eddie Rickenbacker, America's World War I leading flying ace, came to New Orleans to wish us good luck. Shortly thereafter we returned to the barracks and packed our bags.

On May 19, 1942, we traveled to Buffalo, New York, acquiring new P-39s from the Bell plant. We flew them to Grenier Field in Manchester, New Hampshire to await arrival of the 97th Bomb Group whose B-17s were to navigate for us on the Atlantic crossing – one B-17 for each formation of six fighters. This would have marked the first time a fighter group flew the North Atlantic. Mercifully, the trans-Atlantic flight was delayed due to bad weather.

Meanwhile, on the west coast, a Japanese submarine had shelled sites near Santa Barbara, California. As a result, on the 1st of June, we were ordered to fly west in anticipation of a Japanese invasion of our mainland.

Again poor weather intervened precluding departure for the West Coast. In the meantime, General Hap Arnold, now Chief of Staff of the Army Air Forces (the term "Corps" had been officially changed to "Force"), had returned to the U.S. from England. He expressed deep concern over the fact that there were no American Air Force units in the European Theatre. Thus, our orders were modified once again and on June 2nd, Brigadier General Frank O. Hunter, newly appointed head of the Eighth Air Force Fighter Command, came to Grenier Field and addressed all 31st pilots with history-making information.

"Monk" Hunter had been a U.S. fighter pilot in World War I and was a colorful character with a bristling mustache, swagger stick and limited adjectives. He sensed his new command was being raided and his blood pressure ran high. He complained that someone in California claimed they, "saw a goddamned row boat off the coast with a couple of goddamned Japs in it, and the whole goddamned country has gone crazy and sent the whole goddamned Air Force to the West Coast." Monk insisted that "we can beat those goddamned Japs anytime we want to – it's those Germans we have to get after."

Upon departure from New Hampshire, the group received a telegram from General Arnold:

TO 31ST FIGHTER GROUP   GRENIER FIELD
MANCHESTER, NEW HAMPSHIRE
YOU HAVE BEEN CHOSEN TO BE THE SPEARHEAD OF THE U.S. COMBAT FORCES IN THE ETO. CONGRATULATIONS AND GOOD LUCK.
H.H. ARNOLD, COMMANDING GENERAL, ARMY AIR FORCE

Our ground echelon sailed immediately to the United Kingdom on the *Queen Elizabeth* without any naval escort while the pilots caught the next convoy of ships carrying men, material and war supplies to England, leaving behind 80 brand spanking-new P-39s sitting on the ramp in Manchester. Our escorts, the 97th Bomb Group were on the West Coast.

The convoy, comprised of about 40 ships, sailed a zig zag course for twelve days as an evasive measure against German submarines. We had plenty of time to wonder what we were going to do when we got there, considering our P-39s were still in New Hampshire.

2

COMBAT

We made it across the ocean safely, and were received with a tremendous ovation by the British people. Finally, we arrived at Atcham airdrome near Shrewsbury in West Central England. To our astonishment the Brits gave us their own Spitfires! We were stunned. We had our minds set on those shiny, new P-39s and knew little about the British fighter. In fact, future combat experience demonstrated that the replacement of our obsolete P-39s for the Spitfire was a blessing in disguise.

I thought we had another ground looper because of the Spitfire's narrow tread. Yet, during the ensuing year and a half I spent with Spitfires, I never saw one ground loop. I liked the bird from the beginning.

Since we were the first operational fighter group in England, we had frequent visits from dignitaries. Even King George and Queen Elizabeth stopped by and shook hands with and talked to each pilot individually.

Earlier versions of the Spitfire, which were built by Britain's Supermarine Aircraft Company, starred in the Battle of Britain. A multitude of versions followed, ours being the Mark V, or "Spit Five." It was powered by the 1,440 horsepower, twelve cylinder Rolls-Royce Merlin engine, climbed at 3,000 feet per minute and could achieve nearly 460 mph in a dive. It was a very maneuverable airplane and packed a solid punch with its four .303 machine guns and two 20 millimeter cannons.

The Spit did have one frustrating feature. The brakes were actually controlled by a lever on the spade-handle shaped control stick, not the tops of the rudder pedals, to which we were accustomed. You could achieve differential braking by depressing the lever with your hand while simultaneously actuating one rudder pedal or the other, which diverted hydraulic fluid to the brake on the side of the selected rudder pedal. We had a fair share of taxi accidents before we got the hang of it.

To help us acclimate to combat our senior officers flew wing on British counterparts during their first missions. The group's executive officer, Lieutenant Colonel Albert Clark, was flying with a senior British pilot during his first mission when he was shot down over France and taken prisoner by the Germans. How excited the Nazis must have been to capture such a high ranking officer as their first American prisoner of war. We worried that if a pilot that senior and that experienced got bagged his first time out, it was surely going to be a rough war. (Clark survived captivity and went on to an illustrious military career, eventually becoming Commandant of the U.S. Air Force Academy in Colorado Springs, Colorado where he retired as a Lieutenant General.)

Even the war couldn't terminate an important British custom, afternoon tea, a fact that did not sit well with our C.O., Harry Thyng. Harry was short in stature and out of his earshot, was called, with great respect, "Little Man." He was so focused on flight operations that he was adamant against taking a break for ridiculous tea time. His objective was to get us through our training as expeditiously as possible so that we could fly our first combat mission on July 4, 1942, American Independence Day.

Meanwhile, the food was so bad in the Royal Air Force mess (fish for breakfast, mutton and boiled potatoes almost every night for dinner) that after we missed the 4th of July deadline, Harry relinquished the restriction on our participation in tea time. He must have been as plain hungry as we were. As a result, the Americans became the first in line for tea which featured sandwiches, crackers, cookies and jams complementing the otherwise mundane fare.

After twenty-five hours in the Spit and firing no more than fifty rounds of .303 machine gun ammo at a tow target, we were considered battle ready and transferred to Westhampnett near the small town of Chichester, situated along the English Channel close to Portsmouth.

At first, we flew combat air patrols over the Channel to protect against sneak attacks on the airdromes by low-flying Germans who could not be detected by radar. The British high command soon felt that we were ready for more aggressive work and asked the 31st to join with the Royal Air Force in support of a major commando raid on Dieppe, a German occupied seaport on the coast of Northern France. Thus, the 31st became the first American Fighter Group to engage in combat in the ETO.

The raid represented my maiden confrontation with the enemy over occupied France. I had been assigned as wingman to Wing Commander Johnny Walker, scion of the family that produced the famous Scotch whiskey. (I was astonished to learn that Walker's parents had bought him his own personal Spitfire. It cost $20,000 and he used it to fly home on weekends!)

As we walked to our aircraft, Walker cautioned, "Keep your eyes open and stay close to me."

"Yes sir!," I said with enthusiasm, the butterflies buzzing in my stomach. That would be easy advice to follow.

Because the field was entirely grass we were able to take off in increments of as many as a dozen Spitfires all at once. This saved rendezvous time and precious fuel, and was a common practice. Within minutes we were formed and launched toward the Channel.

The most vivid recollection I have of that day was the incredible vista of hundreds upon hundreds of fighters and bombers in the sky, ours and theirs. They were everywhere, swooping and climbing, twisting and turning. Some aflame and plummeting to earth, some entangled in mid-air collisions and a parachute here and there.

I held on for dear life, not a little terrified, and somehow kept up with Johnny Walker. He fired a few times, but I didn't let off a round. I was simply too busy clinging to the leader. I don't know how many near misses there were that day, but I thought, if this was a typical mission, I would never make it through the war. Ninety-one German planes were downed throughout that long day, but about 200 were listed as probables. It was impossible to hang around long enough to confirm a crash. Ninety-eight Allied aircraft were lost, but thirty pilots were saved. Ground units suffered nearly 70 percent casualties, 907 killed, the rest wounded, missing or captured by the Germans.

The commando raid, overall, was a disaster but yielded some valuable information for future invasions. It was the biggest air battle of the war up to that time, and the 31st suffered the loss of eight aircraft and four pilots missing while claiming four kills.

The day after the raid I participated in the largest one-time fighter sweep to date, over LeHavre, France. I was one of more than 500 Allied fighters who filled the sky looking for the enemy. But we didn't stir up a single opponent. If nothing else, the flight constituted a show of force and gave us a chance to flex our aerial muscles, as if to say that our losses the previous day were insignificant.

Even though the British had radar, they had problems controlling so many aircraft in close formation at the same time. It was quite disconcerting while climbing through an overcast in formation to feel the propeller wash of other planes, knowing that another section or squadron of aircraft had just passed in front of yours.

It was during these flights that I gained a full measure of respect for the Spitfire. It didn't have long range capability, but its nifty rate of climb, excellent maneuverability, and high service ceiling were impressive. German Messerschmitt 109s and Focke-Wulf 190s had some advantages over the Spitfire in that they were faster in dives and in level flight. Plus, they invariably knew we were coming and could position themselves to come at us out of the sun. Yet our kill ratio was higher than theirs, even if not by a wide margin.

One day I was sortied to pursue a twin-engined Heinkel 111 observation plane flying over London. We always wore oxygen masks in the Spitfire (the radio transmitter was fitted inside the mask) but we didn't have pressure suits and the cockpits were unpressurized. I climbed for what seemed an eternity to the absolute ceiling of the Spitfire, close to 40,000 feet, and the Heinkel was still flying 1,000 feet above me!

I couldn't coax another foot out of my fighter and the German plane was just ahead, almost mocking me, it seemed. He continued to climb out of gunshot range. I developed a painful case of the bends in my left lower arm which rendered it useless. But it didn't make any difference because I was at full throttle anyway and had reached the limit of my pursuit. In total frustration I pulled the Spitfire up into a stall, aimed at the Heinkel, and fired a long burst from the four machine guns and the 20-millimeter cannon. Predictably, I failed to score any hits. I could do little else but turn back to home base and vent my frustration to my sympathetic British comrades.

Late in October we were transferred by ship to Gibraltar where a fleet of brand new Spitfires was waiting for us. General Jimmy Doolittle, who had flown in from England in a B-17, was the commanding officer of the new Twelfth Air Force and was present during the briefing for the invasion of Africa which would now be our focus of attention.

The new Spits were *desertized*. They were painted tan with a blob of dark brown interspersed here and there, and had larger, protected air scoops to provide more cooling and prevent dust ingestion into the engine. The invading British and American ground troops at Oran in Algeria were experiencing strong opposition from the Vichy French and needed immediate air support. So we were dispatched there.

General Doolittle was a wonder. On November 9, operating out of Tafaroui, confusion reigned. A long column of French Foreign Legion forces were marching toward us, intent on re-taking the airfield. Doolittle rushed out onto the airfield as we maneuvered our Spitfires to take off and attack the advancing column. The general positioned himself on the field so that we could all see him. Like a frantic football coach signaling his charges from the sidelines, Doolittle directed flights of four Spitfires into the air at short intervals, a precaution against collisions on the ground or at low altitude shortly after take-off.

Here was a man already a legend – air racer; the first pilot to take off, fly and land entirely on instruments; holder of many speed records, and leader of the famous raid over Tokyo – right in the midst of action, waving young flyers like me into the sky. That was an unforgettable sight.

The Spits that had no fuel and were left behind were lined up facing the approaching Legion. An enlisted man was in each cockpit ready to fire the plane's machine guns and cannons while two other enlisted men were at the tail, ready to lift it for aiming at the command of the man in the cockpit. To my knowledge, fighters were never used before or since as machine gun nests. Fortunately, this creative approach to combat did not have to be tested.

We lost three aircraft that day but all pilots returned and the Legion was routed. This was considered to be the first time a land force had been destroyed solely by air power.

On November 11, 1942, the French opposition surrendered and when the fury and anger had subsided we asked them why they attacked us. After all, we were their Allies. "It was our honor," they said. "You were invading our country." I still haven't figured out their logic.

Our main function at Oran was to provide close air support for the landing of American troops and to provide air cover for the large convoy of ships carrying men, equipment and food. It wasn't until 33 years later that I learned that my wife's father, who was a chaplain in the Army, was on one of those ships in the harbor. Small world.

After the three-day war with Vichy forces we moved 14 miles north to the main French base at La Senia Airdrome, five miles south of Oran. This was a welcome move because we had been sleeping on the ground and eating unheated C rations. Before evacuating, the French had burned and destroyed all planes and equipment that could not be flown out. The whole airfield was littered with debris. The barracks were adequate but the "johns" were something else that young American boys had never seen. They consisted of two raised footprints and a hole in the floor.

By now each of us had about 20 missions under his belt and while we might have felt like veterans, we were acutely aware of our fragility. On one two-plane scramble to intercept a German bomber I was on my leader's wing when the dust from the dirt field, billowed up by his propeller, created an opaque cloud. I had to stay close to the lead plane because of the poor visibility and my attention was riveted to the outline of his Spitfire. At the lift-off point, I crashed into a previously destroyed French aircraft, which I had not seen, and my Spit flipped end over end into a cartwheel.

There was a god awful sound of cutting, breaking and bending metal. The thought, "I don't want to die! I don't want to die!" whirled through my mind.

Somehow I had the presence of mind to close the throttle, shut off the ignition switch and secure the fuel mixture, to reduce the danger of fire. Still, as I tumbled out of control I believed that this was the end. The Spit came to a halt surrounded by a short-lived cloud of debris. I was dazed to the point of knowing roughly where I was but insufficiently alert to extricate myself from the cockpit. I felt as if I had slammed into a brick wall without any protection.

The airplane was demolished on impact but luckily did not burst into flames. Why an errant spark didn't light the Spit off, I'll never know. Apparently, that mysterious entity called Fate had decided to let me live.

I had slammed into the instrument panel and gun sight and had cut the bridge of my nose and forehead and carved a six-inch U-shaped gash across the top of my head. Ground crewmen pulled me from the wreckage bleeding profusely and dazed as a punch drunk fighter.

Two weeks later I was back on operational duty when the cuts and soreness had healed sufficiently so that I could again wear an oxygen mask and helmet.

I spent several weeks during this period – early 1943 – back in Gibraltar, checking out Spitfires as they came off the assembly line. This signaled the beginning of my test flying experience, although I didn't think of it as such at the time. It usually required two or three hops to iron out the bugs in a new bird. My job was to make the initial flights on the production Spits, check for proper propeller control and rpm, manifold pressure, power output, trim at high speed, instruments, stall speed etc., and then ferry the aircraft to Oran. I made as many as four flights per day.

Hundreds of Spaniards worked on the base and, to get to their jobs, had to cross the airfield, which had no control tower. One day I was scrambled to intercept some German Junker 88 bombers, just as the Spaniards were strolling to work. They hurriedly flopped down on their bellies. Thankfully, the Spitfire didn't need a lot of runway to get airborne, but I narrowly missed mowing down a number of the workers. It's also a good thing I didn't accomplish an intercept with the Ju. 88s because the Spitfire's guns hadn't been tested and their efficiency was in doubt.

My squadron remained in Oran where we enjoyed ourselves as much as we could. The barracks were adequate and wine and champagne were 50 to 75 cents a bottle, respectively. We found an American hospital, but the men outnumbered the nurses about 1,000 to one. So, after a couple of months of flying harbor patrol and intercepting enemy bombers, we were all eager to go to the front and get on with the war.

In the early weeks of 1943, the Germans were pouring troops and supplies into Tunisia from Sicily by sea and by air. Heavy rains hampered the Allied move toward Tunis. In February, the 3lst was ordered to Thelepte Airdrome in Tunisia, 20 miles west of the battle line, where we relieved the 33rd Fighter Group which was flying P-40s. This heavily armored, slow airplane was no match against the more maneuverable and faster German Messerschmitt 109. After landing, I saw a familiar face among the P-40 pilots, and upon approaching him, I recognized Bob Fackler who was a high school classmate of mine and a member of our football team. He said that they had only been at the front for a couple of months, that their losses were high and that they really had a rough time. It was here that I saw a most unusual collection of combat aircraft and pilots spread around the dirt airfield. Americans were flying British Spitfires. The British were flying American A-20s. The French (Lafayette Escadrille Squadron) were flying American P-40s. The field was on a large dirt plateau and was big enough so that each squadron could simultaneously taxi twelve aircraft into take-off position. The entire group of thirty-six ships could be airborne in three minutes. One time we actually made a thirty-six ship formation take-off by tucking the planes in close in a slight echelon to the upwind side. It really raised a dust storm.

Our job was to provide close air support for the ground troops. We flew fighter sweeps, strafed Axis ground forces, and escorted B-17, A-20 and B-25 bombers and P-39 fighter-bombers.

By this time, General "Pistol Packing" Patton had moved from Casablanca to Algiers and was Commanding Officer of the 11th Corps. He was of the firm opinion that most military men were undisciplined and too lax. Orders came down that all personnel would wear helmets, leggings and neckties at all times. This did not boost the morale of the men doing the fighting.

There's a scene in the movie, "Patton," where the general rushes out to the courtyard in Algiers as Nazi planes bore down on his headquarters and started strafing. The general (George C. Scott), in a standing position, bravely draws his Colt .45 caliber pistol and shoots at the attackers. That scene brought a chuckle to me because I had done almost the same thing one morning when we were welcomed to Thelepte by eight strafing Messerschmitt fighters. Admittedly not being as brave or as foolish as the general, I flung myself into a foxhole already occupied by another person.

There was no time to seek another refuge so I just brought my trusty .45 pistol to bear and popped away, with negligible effect, of course. I fired six rounds at one plane while he was firing at least 600 rounds at me with his four machine guns. I missed and fortunately, so did he.

After being at Thelepte only ten days, the enemy was so close that the rumble of its guns was clearly audible. General Rommel's seasoned veterans had moved from Tripoli and begun their offensive against the green and inexperienced American ground forces. It got so bad we were ordered to evacuate the field.

I had my fair share of frightening experiences in the air during the war, but perhaps the most unnerving took place on the ground as we sat in the cockpits of our Spitfires on the darkened airfield at Thelepte, .45 caliber pistols at the ready, waiting for just enough daylight to fly out of there. We dared not launch at night because we feared the airfield could be cratered from the heavy shelling. As we sat there, shadowy figures scurried all about the field, quite near our airplanes. It was impossible to tell who they were, friend or foe. Shells burst in the sky and on the ground, not far away.

Huge fires from burning stores of fuel raged here and there, ignited by our own personnel so that the fuel wouldn't fall into the hands of the enemy, but I didn't know this at the time, adding to my anxiety.

Minutes became hours and the strain was nearly unbearable as the frantic withdrawal continued. At the first hint of dawn, we hurried into the sky and made strafing passes at the advancing Germans until we ran out of ammo and flew to an airfield in Algeria, 45 miles northwest of Thelepte. As the last Spits were taking off, enemy shells were landing in the tent and mess hall areas.

At a flight debriefing, the CO of the French P-40 Lafayette Escadrille rose to speak. I have never seen a man so tormented with grief. He barely managed a word or two, for he was the sole survivor of his squadron of a dozen aircraft. Every other plane had been shot down, every pilot killed, on that terrible day.

The Boche moved into Thelepte Airdrome at 1400 hours the same day that we evacuated. On the following evening, Lord Haw Haw once again gave us his personal attention as he broadcast on the radio for all the world to hear, the infamous lie that the 31st – our Group – had been completely annihilated. He even gave names. But the truth was: not one person – pilot or ground crewman was lost.

In those days, 45 miles from the front lines was a long way to effectively provide ground support to the troops. The Spitfire did not carry enough internal fuel to provide "on station" support. So the engineers carved out a landing strip less than 2,000 feet long, a few miles from the enemy. All we had here was fuel and ammunition. We would go back to the other field at night for rest. This only lasted three days as we were losing more airplanes by nosing up at the end of the short dirt runway while landing than we were from enemy action.

After regrouping, American forces counterattacked. During the Kasserine Pass battle we were escorting, at low altitude, anything that would fly – P-39s, P-40s, A-20s, B-25s and B-26s – conducting as many as three missions a day.

Looking at the ground where the Allied airplanes were laying down a thunderous block bombing attack, I wondered how those poor German bastards could survive such an onslaught.

On March 10th we returned to Thelepte, just three weeks after the inglorious retreat. The German Air Force welcomed our return at dawn the next day by strafing and bombing the field. To add insult to injury, they did it again in the afternoon. Several Spits were damaged, but no one was injured.

Upon returning from a hassle with Me. 109s one day we were jumped by a second flight of enemy fighters with ample fuel while our reserves were dwindling. We were 50 miles from our base. For the entire distance we were caught up in a swirling dogfight with German planes as we tried to work our way home before running out of gas. The Spit wasn't as fast as the Messerschmitt, so we couldn't outrun it.

When we arrived overhead the field, our ack-ack (antiaircraft artillery) came to the rescue. As we landed the Germans withdrew in the face of the ground fire. Most of us just barely made it, nearly flying on fumes.

As a result of this experience, we were forced to maintain a ready alert of manned Spitfires, prepared to take off on a moment's notice.

Three weeks later we again departed Thelepte, but this time it was to pursue rather than escape the enemy.

When operating off one of the dirt fields after a heavy rain, we occasionally encountered difficulties. The day after some rainfall I was asked to taxi the CO's airplane to a different spot. There were puddles of water all over the field, but they did not present a hindrance to taxiing until I hit a deeper and muddier spot. The Spit started to nose over so slowly, it seemed like slow motion. I really didn't think it was going to go all the way onto the prop, but to play it safe, I cut the engine so there wouldn't be a sudden stoppage with the power plant still running. Luck was against me, however, and the aircraft just barely went over onto its nose, damaging the prop. Needless to say, "Little Man" was irate. The hard lesson I learned was very simple: *Never prang the C.O.'s airplane!"*

In early April we were told our aircraft would be gradually replaced with an improved version, the Spit IX, which had a larger and more powerful engine. With it, I could have had a chance at bagging that Heinkel over London. Now, the Me. 109 and the Focke-Wulf 190 would retain their superiority in maximum dive speed *only* – plus a slight edge in maximum level flight speed.

Thirteen days after getting the IXs, I got my first kill. I was flying top cover for a group of fighter bombers when we engaged some Messerschmitt fighters. I latched onto one and started shooting. The projectiles from my four .303 machine guns and two 20-millimeter cannons were converging directly into the area of the cockpit, and the 109 went into an uncontrolled, spiraling dive. I couldn't linger to observe its crash because I had become separated from the rest of my flight and three enemy fighters were converging on me. By continually breaking and turning into their attack all the way home, I was able to save my neck.

On periodic visits to our buddies who flew the P-39s I observed that the pilots were noticeably more jumpy than we were. Reason: their loss statistics were starting to effect them. They were sweating out their 10th or so mission in the P-39 and we all had over 50 sorties in our log books. Our casualty rate for the year-and-a-half I was overseas, including wounded, killed, or captured, was not more than 30 percent.

We weren't enjoying the war by any means, but we found ways to make life tolerable. After flying, we played cards, shot craps, tossed a baseball around, played volleyball, drank French wine and generally, made the most of it. Had our loss rate been worse, our behavior would most assuredly have been different.

As General Rommel's forces retreated toward Tunis, he was able to withdraw most of his antiaircraft artillery. Our missions, therefore became more hazardous due to the heavy ack-ack fire. I really felt for the bomber crews as they had to fly through the clouds of black flak while holding a steady course on bomb runs.

We had the luxury of changing course and altitude, preventing the Germans from drawing a steady bead on us. Even so, my best friend, Harry

Strawn, was shot down off my wing by anti-aircraft fire. It was over three weeks before we heard that he had parachuted to the ground, wounded and been taken prisoner by the Germans. His period of captivity was brief, incidentally. As enemy troops were pushed back to the Mediterranean Sea by Allied forces, they surrendered by the thousands. Strawn said that he had the distinction of accepting the surrender of the German medical unit while he was flat on his back in a hospital recovering from his wounds.

On one mission escorting A-20s, we were attacked by more than twenty enemy fighters. One Me. 109 zoomed fifty feet off my right wing. Unbelievably, I didn't suffer a single hit on my aircraft. He was so close that I could see the pilot, who could have been a rookie and unable to shoot any better than me.

On the same day, on another mission escorting A-20s, we were turned back because of the weather. I saw an A-20 blow up on the field from a fused bomb that fell from its bomb rack. The plane was blasted to smithereens, a grim, sickening sight.

Occasionally, we flew a long mission, escorting bombers out over the Mediterranean to attack enemy supply ships. This required installing a thirty gallon belly tank which gave us another thirty minutes endurance. (By comparison, present day fighters carry 300 gallon auxiliary tanks.)

Eventually, as the Tunisian campaign progressed, the Allies gathered momentum and enemy troops began to retreat to Sicily and points northeast by any method they could contrive. We were dispatched to strafe them, and when I spotted a number of them afloat in row boats and rubber rafts offshore, I simply could not fire at them. To me it would have been like firing at a man in his parachute. Instead, I fired into the water near them, which forced them out of their boats. Then I strafed the boats, sinking them. What happened to the Germans and Italians after that was their problem.

The Germans and Italians surrendered all of Tunisia three days later after my episode with the retreating enemy in their boats and rafts. During the victory parade in Tunis I observed General Charles De Gaulle leading his French troops down the street. Six feet, four inches tall with a distinctive profile, De Gaulle would stand out anywhere, but the picture of this man, brimming with pride as he led, on foot, his ragtag units of French infantry, colonial cavalry (with horses yet), and some ancient tanks and artillery pieces, was memorable.

After nine days of leave in Tunis, I was faced with another move, the ninth in less than four months. We were transferred to the southeastern part of the Cape Bon peninsula to an airfield close to the Mediterranean Sea. At daybreak the next morning, twenty Focke-Wulf 190s and Me. 109s attacked the airdrome and bivouac area. The group suffered its greatest damage from enemy attack this day – ten planes were shot up and twenty-five men were injured, two of whom were my crew chief and armorer.

We began flying again on May 28th with operations focused on Pantelleria Island, 53 miles away, where the Germans and Italians had constructed an underground hangar large enough to house 50 aircraft. The Allied plan was to bomb the island into submission.

For five days our A-20s, B-17s, B-24s, and B-25s bombarded Pantelleria so extensively I wondered how anyone could live through it. After two days there was no enemy air resistance, but the Axis withstood the assault even though the Allies deployed the biggest concentration of bombers up to that time in the war; 1,276 American and British aircraft dropped maximum loads on that tiny island. Pantelleria's white cross on the runway, after five days of bombing just as the landing craft were making their assault on the beaches, signaled the first surrender in military history of land forces to almost purely air forces.

I had often wondered during the Tunisian campaign why I never saw any Italian fighters. I readily found out over Pantelleria when my squadron bagged seven out of twelve Macchi 202s with no loss to ourselves during one mission. I got one of them when I managed to shoot off his left wing. The pilot bailed out. I was so close to him that I had to pull up to avoid hitting the man in his chute.

The day of the surrender also marked one year since our arrival in Great Britain. Our experience was showing. The 31st Group had scored twenty-seven victories with only three losses in three days. This was a vast improvement over the ratio at Dieppe.

On June 30,1943, we moved again, this time to the small island of Gozo near Malta, about 60 miles south of Sicily, as a prelude to the invasion of Sicily itself. The airfield was a short narrow strip transformed from a vineyard in just eleven days. We pranged three airplanes on arrival. One was a wash-out and the pilot was killed.

We were to fly protective cover over an enormous invasion fleet due in early July and to provide air cover for the assault troops on Sicilian soil.

Thankfully, we were living like human beings, inhabiting private homes, sleeping in beds and eating from tables. The Maltese people, made up of Africans, Italians, Spaniards, Syrians, and Greeks, were most interested in what we were doing, and on weekends they came to the airfield in droves to cheer us during take-offs and landings as if we were putting on an air show for them.

On the first mission over the Sicilian beachhead, providing cover for the Allied invasion forces, there was no opposition whatsoever. This was strange because it couldn't have been a surprise attack. We had been escorting bombers over Sicily during the four previous days, softening up the enemy, and there were hundreds of ships in the invasion forces. However, on my second mission on D-day, all hell erupted. The enemy air force timed its attack to strike the ships just as we were leaving because of our low fuel state. We executed a 180 degree turn and pressed back toward the approaching enemy staying in the area as long as we could, but suffered intense ground fire from our friendly forces.

There was probably no other aircraft more easily identified than the Spitfire with its elliptical wing except for the P-38. However, the jittery and trigger-happy American troops on the beachhead and invasion ships were shooting at everything that flew.

Four days after the invasion we escorted C-47s to Sicily where they dropped paratroopers on the airport at Ponte Olivo which we were to occupy. Fortunately, by this time there was no resistance. We became the first American fighter group in Sicily. Here again the situation was similar to that in Oran where we were situated between the main ground forces on the beach and the enemy just eight miles away. Luckily, the enemy was retreating, not advancing.

On the first few missions, we strafed the instant we got our landing gear retracted. The bad guys were that close.

Operations were similar to those in North Africa. We moved three times from airfield to airfield – featuring concrete runways for a change – in close proximity to the front lines. The last enemy forces in Sicily surrendered on 17 August 1943.

By now each of us in the group had logged close to, or more than 100 missions. Replacement pilots began arriving from the States so that some of us could go home. Oddly, the P-39 and P-40 pilots had been cycling back to the U.S. after only 50 missions. They were tasked primarily with strafing missions, especially the P-39s, which exposed them to an awful lot of ground fire. As a result, they lost far more aircraft and pilots than we did in the Spitfires.

While flying out of Termini airdrome on the north side of Sicily along the sea coast 50 miles east of Palermo, I was on ready alert one morning. I was sitting on the ground in my flight coveralls near the planes, chewing the fat with a fellow pilot. We saw a light observation plane approach and land, which was not an unusual occurrence. Some people disembarked, and we paid little attention to them. But a few minutes later a jeep motored by and stopped in front of us. A voice so infused with angry authority that it sent shivers from head to toes, boomed in the air.

"Don't you lieutenants come to attention when the commanding general visits your base?"

We looked up and no more than ten feet away, eyes glaring beneath his helmet, pearl handled pistols gleaming in the sun, stood Lieutenant General George Patton. He had been a passenger on that innocent looking observation plane. In an instant we were cadets again and leapt to quivering attention, saluting on the way up.

We knew Patton was a strict disciplinarian and he certainly lived up to that reputation as far as I was concerned. The look of wrath on his face was message enough and thankfully, he was gone from our presence almost as quickly as he had arrived. We stood in a brace, straight as arrows, until he was well out of sight.

It was shortly after this incident that General Eisenhower severely reprimanded Patton for slapping a GI in a hospital.

The group moved east again, to Milazzo, Sicily, for the invasion of Italy. Our aircraft were now occasionally carrying supplementary 45-gallon gas tanks which increased flight duration from one-and-a-half to two-and-a-half hours. The surviving Germans and Italians who had been defeated in Tunisia and Sicily were regrouping for the defense of Italy, so there was not a lot of air-to-air activity in the days that followed. It wasn't until the actual invasion of Italy commenced on September 3, 1943 that enemy forces took to the air in strength once again.

The 31st Fighter Group was supposed to be the first to land on European soil but the enemy would not cooperate. However, the group's ground echelon landed from LSTs on the Salerno beachhead on September 9th and found themselves caught in a crossfire between British and German artillery. When the artillery eased they were inadvertently bombed by U.S. heavy bombers. It was not until the enemy had been beaten back some three or four miles that the group was able to bring in its airplanes.

This came only after intense fighting at the Salerno beachhead. I did not land in Italy because, on August 31, 1943, I was ordered to return to the U.S. along with a number of other veterans from the 31st. I flew my last mission exactly one year to the day from the Dieppe raid. It consisted of providing air patrol for the convoy steaming for the Italian invasion. We encountered zero enemy aircraft. What a contrast from Dieppe.

A bunch of us from the 31st Group had Distinguished Flying Crosses presented to us by none other than the legendary Lieutenant General "Tooey" Spaatz. Later, back home, when asked why I got the medal, I invariably answered, "For staying alive!" And staying alive meant plenty of "jinking." Jinking means flying in an intentional erratic way – yawing, pitching, rolling – to avoid becoming an easy target for enemy gunners.

Actually, the DFC citation stated that I was leading an element when I spotted four Focke-Wulf 190s coming in at ground level to attack our ground troops in the El Guettar area. We dove in for the attack which caused them to jettison their bombs, without damage, in the no-man's land between the two ground forces.

I locked onto one Jerry and started firing. His plane started to smoke and lose altitude. I was moving in for the kill at about 300 feet above the ground when it seemed as if the battlefield suddenly was ablaze. Enemy ground forces had begun throwing everything but the kitchen sink at us. I knew that I was getting hit by small arms fire because I could hear the bullets thud into the Spit.

I was eyeballing the 190, wanting to see it crash. As I was leaning forward in the cockpit, aligning my gun sight with the 190 for a final burst from my guns, two projectiles slammed through the canopy – one, a 20 millimeter shell from the ground, whizzed by just inches behind my head. I made a spontaneous decision: I forgot about verifying the kill and did what I could to save my own behind.

There is a tried and proven saying in aviation that a 180 degree turn is the best way to get out of bad weather. The same holds true in combat flying. Make the 180-degree turn and get back with the friendlies. I had lucked out again.

In this instance, fate was measured in inches. Erratic jinking, coupled with leaning forward at an unplanned moment prevented an enemy round from blowing my head off.

Summarizing, the reliability of the Spit's Merlin engine was excellent even while flying in the African desert. I had one aborted flight in the Spitfire due to the engine overheating from a glycol leak and another from a partial loss of manifold pressure. I was only hit twice – once from ground fire and once in the air from an adversary whom I didn't see. I had five airplanes personally assigned to me. Four of them were shot down and one crash landed – all with other pilots at the controls. To this day I ask the unanswerable question: Why did Lady Luck shine on me?

3

WRIGHT FIELD

After leaving Dayton, Ohio as a neophyte airman I arrived back home for the first time in almost two-and-a-half years as a seasoned combat veteran. I enjoyed a 30-day leave period, most of which I spent at home with my folks. Then I was sent to a rest and recreation facility in Atlantic City to await further orders. In Atlantic City I roomed with Captain Dale Shafer, another Mediterranean vet.[1] We stayed in a luxury hotel on the beach and one morning we were awakened by machine gun fire. I instinctively leaped out of bed and ducked under it. I glanced beneath the other bed and sure enough, Dale was there. We both felt sheepish when we learned that the Navy had a gunnery range out over the ocean just outside our hotel.

While in Atlantic City we put in our preferences for our next assignment. We had no illusions about getting our choices, knowing that "needs of the service" always prevailed. For example, I had always requested multi-engine training but always wound up in single-engine planes. Still, I had given some thought to the forthcoming orders.

I had developed such a keen admiration for the Spitfire that whenever I was asked about its capabilities, I replied, "It was the perfect airplane for the Battle of Britain. And no one should ever get shot down in a Spit unless he's attacked by an unseen foe."

Anyway, the Spitfire's fundamental simplicity and its wonderful handling characteristics were so praiseworthy that I began to think of ways that I could contribute to the war effort by incorporating the aircraft's favorable features into our Army Air Force planes.

Army Air Force test and development work was conducted at Wright Field. While in Dayton on leave, I expressed interest to some people on the base about assignment to Wright. None gave me any encouragement. In those days it was unheard of to be stationed in your own home town. Additionally, I had not gotten my degree in aeronautical engineering because I left college after three years to join the Army Air Corps.

But there was an opening in the Special Weapons Group and I pursued it. I applied for the billet, thinking that I could later manage a transfer to Fighter Flight Test.

The Special Weapons Group was the forerunner of others that dealt with guided missiles, smart bombs and such. I was exhilarated when orders came through assigning me to the group in November 1943. I had now come full cycle in two-and-a-half years, from a junior draftsman at $80 per month to a "test pilot" making $450 a month!

During the time I was stationed at Wright Field, I felt like the richest captain in the Army Air Force. I was living at home (my parents were so happy to have me in Dayton they insisted that I not pay any room or board); I was receiving an allowance for quarters plus subsistence pay, not to mention my regular and flying pay; I would be traveling on TDY assignments, receiving per diem in the process; and I was single. On top of that, my only possessions were my Buick, a parachute bag stuffed with flight gear and a B-4 bag jammed full of uniforms. In short, I was drawing great money and had no debt burden.

After my first week in the Special Weapons Group, I flew as copilot with Captain Bob Cardenas[2] on a B-17 to Muroc Air Base in the California desert where B-24 flight crews trained. At the North Base, on the upper end of this enormous dry lake, there was a hangar housing super secret projects under Wright Field purview.

As we taxied in from the lake bed I saw a strange looking aircraft sans propeller. We shut down, and as I looked out I asked the sergeant who was chocking the wheels of the B-17, "What kind of an airplane is that?"

"That's a jet," he said.

Perplexed, I inquired, "What's a jet?"

"It's a plane without props," he replied.

"Oh, I see."

He explained that it was a Bell P-59 and that it was undergoing flight testing. That was my first exposure to the new technology which was to play a major role in my life. I didn't learn much else about the airplane due to the clandestine nature of the project. In the days that followed, we proceeded with our testing, and the P-59 people continued with theirs.

At Muroc our project consisted of a 2,000 pound bomb attached to a wing featuring a 20 foot span designed to extend its glide distance. At 10,000 feet altitude, we flew the B-17 toward the lake bed. At a point 20 miles away, we let loose the inert, unguided, glide bomb.

We managed to hit the target satisfactorily, but the commander of the B-24 training base became queasy about winged bombs soaring through his airspace. So he "banished" us from further destruction of the lake bed.

Living conditions at Muroc were horrible. We ate out of mess kits, and our barracks consisted of partially walled off sections without doors. Howling winds deposited sandy dust all over everything. We hated the situation so much that almost every other night we drove three hours to Hollywood where we raised a little hell, then took turns driving back to Muroc, catching a few winks on the way.

On the west side of the main Muroc Air Base there was a small bar and restaurant called "Panchos Happy Bottom Riding Club". It was an OK place to have a beer and dinner, but being only 22 years old I wanted the bright lights of Hollywood. There was no black-out in the States at this time during the war as there had been in England, and I had enough of the desert during my tour in North Africa.

The Happy Bottom Riding Club was established in 1941 and grew as the war went on. Muroc Army Air Field became the site for B-24 and B-25 aircrew training, so there were customers aplenty. I didn't actually frequent the Club until 1950 when I was on steady assignment at Muroc.

When I returned to Wright Field after six weeks at Muroc, I requested an audience with the CO, told him about the miserable living conditions and added, "I'd rather be sent back overseas than return to Muroc."

He didn't like that very much, told me I would have to make do, and sent me back to the desert in January 1944, only this time to Tonapah, Nevada, on a heat-seeking bomb project using a B-25 aircraft.

Huge bonfires were lit out in the desert and a heat-seeker in the nose of the bomb would home in on the heat radiating from the bonfire. The project was fairly successful and it is believed that the principle derived from this concept was the forerunner of the heat-seeking Sidewinder missiles that are carried on modern jet fighters.

Tonapah was a small mining town about halfway between Las Vegas and Reno. There was a house or two of ill repute located there along with several bars and a few shops, not exactly a prime place for rest and relaxation. Every weekend, therefore, we packed up the B-17 with our supporting crews and flew to Reno or Las Vegas for a taste of more sophisticated night life.

At the completion of this project and a short stay at Wright Field, I was assigned to another special weapons project. This time we went to a remote base at Wendover, Utah, on the border with Nevada and west of the great Salt Lake.

The test project had to do with a radio-controlled (azimuth only) bomb, whose acronym was RAZON. The test team consisted of three military men: myself, Captain Chiba, the bombardier, and a sergeant who acted as copilot on the B-17 during the flight tests. The other four members were civilian engineers with two assigned to Wright Field. The remaining two were contractor personnel.

The flight test plan called for a climb to 25,000 feet where we would drop the bombs and guide them into the target by radio signals. The visual acquisition of the bomb was provided all the way to the target by attaching 1,000,000 candlepower flares to it. These ignited when released from the bomb rack.

One day, one of the bombs hung up partially in the bomb rack, but it had moved enough to ignite the flare which lit other flares. Soon the entire bomb bay was a blazing inferno. Like fire in a ship, fire in an airplane spells disaster. There was no time to ponder.

"Bail out!," I ordered. "Everybody bail out!"

The four civilians and Captain Chiba went through the lower hatch, and I was in the process of leaving the pilot's seat for my own escape when I glanced aft and saw the sergeant, in the area behind the flight deck, struggling to adjust his parachute which was too small for him. He had borrowed it from someone else and had neglected to set the straps for his body before we left the ground.

Since we were at 25,000 feet, I realized that the sergeant would soon pass out for lack of oxygen because he had left his mask in the copilot's seat. A thought raced through my mind: What do I do with an unconscious man in an ill-fitting parachute in an airplane with the entire bomb bay aflame?

I resettled in the pilot's seat, pulled the four throttles to idle, and pushed the Flying Fortress into a steep dive. I had to get to a lower altitude before the sergeant passed out.

We hurried down to 10,000 feet, the B-17 whistling noisily through the air, the airframe buffeting wildly through the sky because the bomb bay doors were open. When I looked back, the sergeant had successfully adjusted his chute, and for some wonderful, crazy reason, the fire had extinguished itself.

"Sir, should I bail out now?" asked the sergeant urgently.

"No, no," I said, astonished. "Not now. Get back up here and help me land this thing."

Fortunately, I made my smoothest landing ever in the B-17. Had I botched it, or come in unsteadily, the aircraft might have broken in half because the main bulkhead in the bomb bay had nearly burned through.

Ironically, two of the four who bailed out broke their legs after landing in the rocky hills surrounding Wendover. During their recovery they chided me for ordering the emergency bailout while I was too chicken to go "over the side" myself.

There is no light quite as bright as the white phosphorous from a high candlepower flare, especially up close. Over fifty years after this precarious moment in the sky I recall it so vividly it could have happened yesterday.

I spent a lot of time in the western desert during the year I was in the Special Weapons Group, but whenever I returned to Wright Field I dropped in on the Fighter Test Section, hoping to make a connection that might lead to an assignment there. I had become a little disenchanted flying multi-engine aircraft and testing special weapons. I yearned to get back into fighters. I wanted to pursue my objective of advocating lighter and simpler American fighter aircraft. Luckily, with the help of Captain Wally Lein, a slot came open for a captain and I got the job.

One of my first assignments in fighters in late 1944 was to check out in Bell's P-59 Aerocomet jet. It was the only one on the base and was the same type of aircraft I had seen a year before during that B-17 trip to Muroc in California. The P-59 had straight wings with inlet ducts near the wing roots and was driven by a pair of General Electric turbines which produced 1,600 pounds of thrust per engine. Although I was intrigued with flying an aircraft without a propeller – one that flew smoothly and sounded totally different from the reciprocating types I was used to – that first flight was far from routine.

I climbed out to 12,000 feet and cruised around all over Dayton, anxiously seeking out a P-47, a P-51, or any prop aircraft, which I could sneak up on and fly formation with to see the look of surprise on the pilot's face when he saw my propeller-less flying machine. Alas, there was no one available. After awhile I got my share of excitement, however, when one of the engines quit. The P-59 was far from a great performer with two engines. With one, it was a flying brick, and I was barely able to keep it in the sky.

I immediately headed back for the base and made it down safely but have to admit that the approach and landing produced far more anxiety than I had experienced in reciprocating planes under similar circumstances.

Only fifty production models of the P-59 were produced and they never saw combat. It was replaced by the Lockheed P-80 two-and-a-half years later. The P-80 had a 4,000 pound thrust engine and was a significant improvement over its predecessor.

The Air Force soon realized that its test pilots and design engineers were not communicating very well. The pilots were employing terms like "squirrely," "weird," and "wild and snakey," which the engineers didn't understand. This was a prime reason the Air Force established its Test Pilot School (TPS) in late 1944 to teach the pilots how to fly performance, stability and control tests, and also how to employ proper terminology in reporting to the engineers.

For example, with the advent of the jet and high indicated airspeeds, the longitudinal control on some airplanes became quite sensitive. A North American pilot was tooling along at high speed and low altitude when those monitoring the flight by radio heard the pilot suddenly exclaim, "Jesus Christ!" and that's all.

On the ground he told them that the airplane almost broke up because of sensitive control, and he was out of phase in trying to control it. He took his hands off the controls and let the aircraft damp in pitch by itself. This incident became famous in the test pilot's vocabulary as the "J.C. Maneuver." Whereas in the engineer's vernacular it is correctly described as "a pilot-induced oscillation which caused a short period of divergent pitching accelerations." Maybe we should have had the engineers learn our language instead of the other way around.

Importantly, during my new assignment, I was selected to attend the second U.S. Air Force Test Pilot School class in company with legendary pilots – Major Dick Bong, Captain Don Gentile, and Captain Glen Edwards – all noteworthy World War II heroes. There was a shortage of space at Wright Field so the school was moved temporarily to Vandalia Municipal Airport in Dayton where we flew and held our classes. It was moved to Patterson Field in late 1945 and eventually to Edwards Air Force Base in 1951.

On a typical day we would study aerodynamics and other subjects for half a day in the classroom then spend the other half in the sky, putting to work what we had learned on the ground. I was not a great student in college, just managing to get by with satisfactory grades but I felt I was in my element at TPS and really applied myself. I got some good grades but more importantly, I started learning how to gain maximum performance out of an airplane. Thus, TPS was an experience of great significance to me personally, and I valued it throughout my career.

My first assignment after TPS graduation involved the Republic P-47. I soon learned first-hand what it really meant to develop a dislike for an airplane. Any military pilot who has survived a combat tour thinks his airplane "is the best," no matter what he flew. I have had many P-47 pilots expound on the ruggedness and reliability of the Thunderbolt. But I had four flights in the plane over a period of less than four weeks, totaling less than a collective four hours, and each of these flights culminated in one form of an emergency or another.

The first sortie ended after an hour because a caution light illuminated indicating low fuel. Because of a faulty transfer valve I could not use any of the gas from other tanks so I descended immediately and made it to the runway, but the engine quit on roll-out due to fuel starvation.

On the second hop, shortly after take-off, I experienced severe power loss and had just enough airspeed and power to execute a gentle bank over the tree tops to achieve a downwind, cross wind landing. I skimmed over

31

the Wright Field hangars and got the wheels down and locked a fraction of a second before contacting the runway. The flaps were still in the process of lowering and the throttles had not been touched to reduce power. I landed using all available power. Gulp!

On the third flight, in a P-47N, while conducting a water injection (war emergency power) engine test at high altitude, I had another problem. Everything was "in the green" during the first test, but suddenly the engine simply quit running. Since the airplane was highly instrumented and the data gained of significant value for combat crews who would be conducting long range missions in the Pacific, I had no thought of bailing out, trusting that I could dead-stick it to a landing at the airfield.

Wrong! Instead, I had to belly it in wherever possible. As I worked my way down, stretching the glide to reach a small bean field, I could hear the warnings of my primary flight instructor from four years ago ringing in my ears: "Don't stall! Don't ever stall!"

I made the bean field all right but with the gear retracted, had too much altitude due to low drag. Proceeding across the field I found myself aimed directly at the farmer's house. At the last second I kicked in full right rudder, skewing the Thunderbolt to miss the house, knowing I would end up in an adjacent stand of trees. I slammed into one large tree after another, cutting the fuselage in half just behind the cockpit and knocking off a wing, part of the other wing and stopping just three feet short of a big tree in front of the engine. I felt like the ball in a pin ball machine as I bounced from tree to tree. If the fuselage had struck the tree a hair of a second earlier, I would have been squashed flat as a pancake.

The P-47N was demolished. The biggest piece remaining from the calamity was the engine and the cockpit with young Captain Bob Rahn still aboard. Miraculously, my only injury was a scratched thumb where the control stick had broken off in my hand.

When the farmer and his wife came upon the wreckage I was slumped over in the cockpit, thanking God for letting me live. I looked up and calmly said, "Would you mind calling Wright Field for me?"

The woman fainted because she figured I had died in the crash. Helped out of the cockpit by the farmer, I headed back to the farm house and made the call myself. Since it was Sunday morning, I had to wait some time to be picked up and asked if I could lie down on their couch. Whereupon I dozed off, much to their astonishment.

On my fourth flight in the P-47, an air show demonstration, I was "shot down" by Major Dick Bong, leading American ace in World War II with forty victories who was piloting a Lockheed P-38 Lightning. We were in a staging area at Wright Field waiting to make individual passes over the runway and had time to kill, so Dick said, "Let's have a little dog-fight." I nodded and we went at it.

Within minutes he was on my tail, and I heard the transmission no fighter pilot wants to hear:

"Bang, bang, bang, you're dead!" Bong really knew how to fly that Lightning.

I checked out in all the fighters at Wright Field at the time and had an absolute ball doing it. In fact, my younger brother, who was an airplane buff and who had built models of some of the planes I flew, got to see them up close. Our house in Dayton was located just on the edge of the city limits. In those days we were allowed to fly acrobatics and perform other test work in the area as long as we didn't infringe on the city limits.

I would take off from Wright, work my way over to the house, and then perform a series of acrobatics – an air show in miniature, if you will – for the benefit of my brother, who enjoyed the sight immensely.

This went on for a half dozen hops in different airplanes until complaints from the neighbors arrived at the base commander's desk, and I was summoned on the carpet. He pointed out that I had become a nuisance due to the regularity of my appearances in the same geographic location.

"But sir," I explained, "I'm entirely legal and within the rules."

"That may be," said the CO, "but sometimes that's not good public relations."

He slapped me on the wrist with a letter of admonition, which ended the air shows, but it was fun while it lasted.

I was allowed to take military passengers along for a ride when flying a two-seat aircraft, and once I took my childhood buddy, Howard Beck, aloft in a P-61 Black Widow. Howard had logged some flight time as a student in the Navy's training command, so I let him fly the airplane. At one point he dove down to gain some speed, then pulled up to perform a loop. We were "on top," inverted, but the Black Widow stalled and began to enter a spin.

"OK, Bob," Howard said with admirable nonchalance, "you've got it."

Well, I took it and after some energetic maneuvering, made the recovery. I had only one or two flights in the P-61 and got to thinking, "This isn't exactly a smart thing to do." Had there been an accident and had we survived, I wouldn't have come out of the investigation very well.

I also got to evaluate the P-38L and P-51H, which were the late models of the respective aircraft. Interestingly, in July, 1945, two "new boys" reported to Flight Test – Chuck Yeager and Bob Hoover, destined to be a pair of aviation's most honored and accomplished aviators. Yeager, a World War II ace, later won worldwide renown. Hoover was also a Spitfire pilot, became a prisoner of war, and is a flyer of immense skills who continues to be a singularly noteworthy member of today's air show circuit.

During my tour with the Special Weapons Group I had visited the Douglas Aircraft plant at Mines Field in Los Angeles (now Los Angeles International Airport) to borrow a B-17 from a civilian contractor which we needed for some test work. I was amused by the fact that the Army Air Force was borrowing a military airplane from one contractor that had been manufactured by another. It was there that I met and befriended Bob Brush, Douglas' Chief Test Pilot, who asked me to keep in touch with him on what I was doing.

Shortly after graduating from TPS I received a telegram from Brush in which he offered me a job as a test pilot for Douglas. The company was working on an attack aircraft designated the XBT2D which he thought I would be well suited to fly.

It was more than two weeks before I responded. I had an envious position at Fighter Test and was certainly pleased with my lot. At the same time, I didn't think I wanted to stay in the service, as I still had it in the back of my mind that when the war was over I would become an airline pilot and fly multi-engine aircraft. Bob's telegram got my mind to churning, and presented me with a quandary.

For the time being, I felt I was doing what was best for my country by applying what skills and ideas I possessed toward improving the aircraft our guys were flying on the front lines. The more I considered Brush's offer, however, the more I was drawn to the idea of accepting it.

I had enough combat missions, overseas time and points under the military's system of duty credit that I could leave the Air Force for a position in an "essential" industry, which Douglas Aircraft certainly was. Reasoning that I would be able to accomplish more toward improving aircraft at Douglas than I could at Fighter Test, I began leaning toward the industry offer. I certainly wanted more flight time, and I had no desire to "fly a desk," take an administrative position, or train cadets in the Air Force.

Also, I was lured by the fact that Douglas Aircraft at the time was the General Motors of the aviation industry, a big, growing and successful company which turned out quality products. They made fighters, attack planes, bombers, cargo aircraft, and commercial transports.

I was also attracted to Douglas because of its location. They had major plants at El Segundo, Long Beach, Torrance, Culver City and Santa Monica in Southern California. In 1944 when I flew into Mines Field where the Douglas plant at El Segundo was located, I stayed over for a couple of days. I had gone skiing in the local mountains in the morning and swimming in Palm Springs in the afternoon. Coming from Ohio, that really impressed me. "This is the place I want to live after the war," I said to myself.

My mind made up, I contacted Brush, told him that I would accept the job, made the necessary arrangements at Wright Field to be released from the service, packed a suitcase and took to the highway in my cream-colored Buick convertible. I drove to Douglas's Santa Monica, California plant, where I reported for work on August 2, 1945.

1. Shafer later became a Major General of the Ohio National Guard.
2. He later did considerable evaluation flying in Northrop's B-49 Flying Wing and became a Brigadier General.

4

EARLY DAYS AT DOUGLAS

I expected to check out in the XBT2D right away. A couple of days after arrival, however, I was assigned to fly the BTD. It was a gull-winged plane driven by the Wright R-3350 which produced 2,250 horsepower. My performance in the BTD, presumably, would give Bob Brush an idea of my ability to evaluate a new airplane. I wasn't impressed with the BTD. I put it through some rolls, loops and Immelmanns and in my report, wrote, "The control forces are quite heavy and one has to be a very strong man to do acrobatics in this airplane."

I did reasonably well in my first stint as a civilian test pilot, but it turned out the Navy wasn't impressed with the BTD any more than I was. Only thirty were built and further orders were canceled.

Two days later I flew as copilot in a B-17, to Wendover Air Force Base in Utah on a special weapons project called the ROC. "What had I gotten myself into?" I wondered. I was supposed to be test-flying Douglas' new attack aircraft. Instead, I was operating a heavy-duty B-17 and testing special weapons again. Thankfully, this assignment only lasted a few days and we returned to Los Angeles.

A little later, to my surprise, I was sent on a check flight of sorts in a four-engine C-54 transport, flying from the left seat. I had absolutely no experience in the multi-engine cargo ship. Indeed, I had never been in it before. Not surprisingly, I did poorly in the lumbering machine because I had no opportunity to even get acquainted with the layout of the cockpit, or read the manual. Considering its four engines , the C-54 had sixteen basic engine controls, thirty-two ancillary switches and thirty-two instruments to inform the crew of the status of each engine. But my airmanship must have been reasonably satisfactory because I wasn't fired and continued in the employ of Douglas Aircraft.

Meanwhile, the company maintained high hopes for the XBT2D attack plane, then known as the Dauntless II, later to be the Skyraider. Laverne "Tailspin Tommy" Browne, an absolutely terrific gentleman and pilot – and my hero from teenage Saturday-afternoon-matinee-days – had made the first flight in the aircraft, the developmental XBT2D, in the spring of 1945. I had been with the company nearly a month before checking out in the airplane which I had originally been hired to fly.

Unknown to me at the time, Bob Brush felt that "Brownie" was getting on in years and needed some help in the structural and aerodynamic demonstration testing of the aircraft. He wanted young blood to replace older men like Tailspin Tommy and specifically sought combat-experienced pilots like myself. George Jansen, for example, was hired the day after I signed on, and Jack Armstrong came in a few months later. Bob particularly liked the fact that I had completed test pilot school at Wright Field.

35

My initial pay as a test pilot was 450 dollars a month, the same as an Army Air Force captain. Assuming I succeeded during the six-month probationary period, I would be advanced to the status of an experimental test pilot at 600 dollars a month. *Production* test pilots made less because they flew airplanes which had already undergone experimental testing. Production test flights were designed to verify that the systems and flight characteristics, which had been initially developed by the experimental test pilots, were functioning properly.

True to the legend which surrounded the beginnings of the plane, the XBT2D was partially conceived overnight in a Washington DC hotel room in June 1944. The great Ed Heinemann, Chief Engineer at Douglas' El Segundo plant, and two senior assistants, had frantically refined the design of the aircraft already laid out for the R-2800 engine in general perspective. The Navy subsequently decided it wanted the R-3350 engine to power the aircraft, so the trio labored 'til the wee hours working up blueprints, in order to meet an 0900 Navy deadline next morning. They succeeded and as a result, the aircraft which was destined to become a mainstay in the Navy, Marine Corps, Air Force, and the air service of several foreign nations was born. Among the names it was eventually know by were: Flying Dump Truck, Pedigreed Pulverizer, Big Machine, and Spad.

It was a low-wing cantilever monoplane with a wing span of 50 feet and a gross wing area of 400 square feet. All-metal ailerons with trim and balance tabs were used as were single-slotted trailing edge flaps. The thick wing gave a maximum lift coefficient of 2.0, an excellent characteristic.

The fuselage was an all-metal monocoque structure thirty-eight feet, ten and one-half inches in length, featuring an integral fin standing twelve feet high. Dive brakes were components of the fuselage. There was one on each side and one on the bottom of the fuselage, all hydraulically actuated. (The concept of the fuselage dive brakes was originally developed on the BTD.) The brakes were very effective and held the airplane safely under 300 mph in a vertical dive.

The empennage consisted of all-metal control surfaces with an electrically-controlled, adjustable horizontal stabilizer. The rudder and elevator were aerodynamically and statically balanced, with trim and spring tabs on the rudder to reduce control forces. The landing gear system, a conventional type with a tail wheel, was hydraulically actuated. (The conventional system was lighter than the tricycle type characterized by a nose wheel and two main mounts.) The aircraft was powered by the massive Wright R-3350-24 featuring eighteen cylinders arranged in twin rows with nine cylinders per row – one row behind the other. The air-cooled engine was rated at 2,400 horsepower with a single-stage, two-speed supercharger. Later versions of the engine (-26W) produced 2,700 horsepower. The propeller, made by Aeroproducts, was a four-blade, constant speed, hydraulically-actuated, variable pitch control prop with a sizable diameter of thirteen and one-half feet.

A single, leak-proof fuel cell with a capacity of 380 gallons occupied the entire cross sectional area of the fuselage just aft of the pilot. Armament consisted of two 20-millimeter cannons, rocket launchers, and bomb or torpedo racks. The empty weight of the aircraft – without fuel and stores – was only 10,470 pounds.

On my twelfth flight in the prototype, the XBT2D, I was tasked with a relatively simple test to demonstrate the design criteria of the bomb ejector. A shotgun-type shell installed in the ejector rack on the centerline station on the bottom of the fuselage was electrically fired from the cockpit, *kicking* the weapon away from the airplane and sending it on its way to the target. I was to climb to altitude, enter a 90-degree dive and release a 2,000 pound inert bomb. According to the engineers, the bomb was supposed to clear the propeller by 12 inches. I was to hold the dive for several seconds after release so that a wing-mounted camera could photograph the bomb/propeller clearance.

The opening chapter of this book described the debacle of this flight and my unusual exit from the disabled Dauntless II. Parachuting into the Pacific was only part one of the problem.

Since this was an afternoon flight and matters had deteriorated too quickly for me to notify rescue elements, I was on my own. What I wouldn't have given for a chase plane. Floating in the water I evaluated my plight. I was approximately eight miles off shore from El Segundo and knew that it would be some time before the company realized that an emergency had occurred and sent help. But I did have a life jacket with a dye packet which I released. The dye-marker created a large, light green circle in the blue Pacific ocean.

I floated there, within the circle, waiting for rescue moving as little as possible because I didn't want to attract any sharks or cause the spread of the dye-marker spot.

I saw nothing, boat or airplane, for about an hour and with each passing minute got a little more anxious. I was a fair swimmer and felt I could hold on for some time, but I was running out of daylight. Fortunately, I hadn't become shark bait. At one point, as I rode up the crest of a wave and looked eastward, I saw the lights coming on along the shoreline, signaling the inevitable descent of darkness. Patience gave way to the instinct for survival.

Reasoning that I was in good physical shape, and it didn't appear anyone was yet on the way to assist me, I started swimming, hoping the sharks were busy elsewhere.

To my great relief, after about fifteen minutes of the Australian crawl, I heard the drone of an aircraft overhead. A North American P-82 Double Mustang flew over me. I had been spotted. I learned later the pilot was on a production test flight. Shortly thereafter I was the focus of attention as rescue forces hurried into action. In addition to the P-82, a Douglas DC-4 and a Coast Guard boat converged. The Coast Guard crewmen hauled me aboard and hustled me ashore where it was dark when I arrived.

The company doctor and others were waiting for me at the dock and promptly whisked me off to Douglas' medical center for examination. I tried my best to eliminate this formality for two reasons. I felt fine but most of all, I had a blind date and tickets to the UCLA vs. USC football game that evening.

By the time I finished the medical exam and gave my account of what happened to company officials, the game was half over. I had left my date's name and number at home so couldn't contact her. Much later that evening, after the formalities with the company were finished, I called her and explained that I had bailed out of an airplane and was in the ocean for a long time. I don't think she believed me and didn't contact her until twenty-five years later.

I was at a cocktail party and overheard a group talking about unusual situations they had experienced in their life times. A middle-aged lady began describing a blind date who never showed up and had a whopper of a tale about bailing out of an experimental airplane and being in the ocean for a long time before being rescued. Stunned, I sidled up to the lady and introduced myself, explaining that I was the guy who had told her that story 25 years earlier. It was worth the wait just to see the look of astonishment on her face. In any case, for my achievement that day, I could probably have made it into the Guinness Book of Records as pilot of the only plane to have been shot out of the sky by its own bomb.

On the numerous occasions that I flew the BT2D from California to the Navy's test facility at Patuxent River, (Pax), Maryland, I tried to land at Wright Field in Dayton, my home town, to stay overnight, visit with Air Force friends at the base and, of course, my folks. At Wright Field I would inevitably encounter one of my Air Force pals, Dick Bong, Chuck Yeager, Bob Hoover, or Don Gentile, to name a few. They would be in the sky in a P-51, P-38, or what have you, ready to pounce on me.

Whoever it was would invariably intercept my BT2D, then proceed to execute barrel roll after barrel roll around my airplane, enticing me to engage in a dog fight. Every instinct in my body said counterattack! I was sorely tempted to engage them. The BT2D may have been an attack bomber, but it had considerable agility. My particular aircraft, however, was fully instrumented for test work and had a one million dollar price tag on it. There would be hell to pay if something went wrong during one of these playful pursuits. So my Air Force comrades had their fun while I watched, frustrated but enjoying the show.

When I ferried the first model of the BT2D to Pax in January 1946 for demonstration tests, I was met by a sizable crowd of people, including the top brass, all intensely interested in the new flying machine, and was deluged with questions even before I climbed out of the cockpit.

"How maneuverable is it?"

"How does it handle?"

"What bomb load does it carry?"

"What are the performance figures?"

These questions I could handle. Then someone asked, "What are the wave-off characteristics?"

I was perplexed. I didn't know what he meant.

"What's a wave-off?" I asked. Curious expressions came over the faces around me. In the Air Force if we couldn't land for one reason or another, we executed a "go-around." When the Navy's carrier wave-off was explained to me I was so embarrassed I wanted to crawl into the hell hole of the BT2D and hide.

The diagram displays the Vn (velocity – load factor), or "flight envelope," as it is often called, for a Skyraider with a gross weight of 15,600 pounds. Each type of aircraft has its own Vn diagram. It is a key tool for all aviators and depicts the limiting structural parameters of the respective aircraft. The diagram is created by design engineers and demonstrated or "proved" by the experimental test pilot before the aircraft is turned over to the customer.

The preliminary dives needed to attain the figures on the right-hand side of the Vn curve had been performed on the prototype XBT2D, which was lost in the bomb collision. Consequently, we didn't take the new airplane to its design limits at the factorybefore going to the Navy Test Center at Pax.

On my 13th test flight there I was climbing out to the restricted dive test area in aircraft number 088 with an inert 2,000 pounder slung on the centerline rack. The purpose of the dive was to demonstrate the strength of the bomb ejector when 7 Gs were imposed with a ton of ordnance on the rack. In order to do this, a fuel tank had to be removed so that the gross weight of the airplane with the bomb would not exceed 15,600 pounds. Thus, I had only a partial fuel supply on take-off.

While in my ascent the engine suddenly sputtered and quit, as if I had run the fuel tank dry. I tried frantically to restart the engine. All gauges were "in the green" before the power plant stopped running, and the fuel gauge indicated I had plenty of fuel. Unfortunately, I was too far from the base and didn't have enough altitude to glide back to the air station, even though I jettisoned the bomb to lighten the aircraft.

There was no suitable landing field within sight so I put the aircraft down, wheels up, in a bean field, skidding to a stop just short of a wooded area. The airplane was repairable but not to the extent that it could still be used to continue the demonstration tests.

Subsequent investigation by the Navy revealed a faulty fuel gauge, which read more than half full when in reality, the tank was empty. Worst of all, officials blamed me and described the cause as pilot error. I protested that conclusion because I always conscientiously performed my walkaround, or preflight inspection, of any airplane before each flight.

However, it was not my procedure nor that of any other test pilot to "dipstick" the fuel tanks. I customarily relied upon the crew chief to handle this function. Reluctantly, I did not contest the decision, reasoning, "the customer is always right."

Another plane was assigned to complete the formal tests at Pax. It was the first production model and was called the AD-1. The A represented Attack, the D, Douglas, the 1, the first model or version. Since the production plane was supposed to be exactly the same configuration as the prototypes there was no difference between the -1 and its predecessor, the BT2D. The popular name was also changed to Skyraider which was the first of Douglas' fabled "Sky" series of airplanes.

When it came to structural testing of the aircraft in those days, only a preliminary dive in California to 80 percent of the design load factor was required before final tests at Pax. These tests came under the category: PLAA (plus low angle of attack).

On my first dive at Patuxent, when I pulled 7 Gs at maximum speed, about ten feet of skin pulled away from the rear spar on the right outer wing panel. It was more expeditious to fly a new wing out from the plant in El

Segundo than to repair the damaged one. Since the limit dive speed (VL) of 500 mph was not attained on this flight, I experimented with several types of dive entries to determine the best way to accelerate. These included the split S, roll-in entry, or zero lift pushover. The zero lift pushover proved to be the optimum maneuver for this purpose and was ideal in that it allowed more precise control in achieving the required dive angle.

For the demonstration maneuver, I climbed to 27,500 feet, the combat ceiling of the Skyraider (the height at which the aircraft can no longer climb at 500 feet per minute with military power), pushed over into a 70-degree dive angle and held it until initiating pull-out at 8,000 feet. I recovered to level flight at 4,800 feet. The pullout was satisfactory, with reasonable control stick forces, but the maximum indicated airspeed (IAS) attained was only 487 mph.

Once again, the structural design limit speed of 500 mph was not attained. By the time 7 Gs had been applied, the speed had dropped off to 483 mph.

There were meetings at the Naval Bureau of Aeronautics (BuAer) in Washington, DC to work out a technique to achieve the upper limit of the Vn which was 500 mph and 7 Gs. Officials said that since limit dive speed was not attained in a 70-degree dive, the new requirement would be a 90-degree dive starting from service ceiling (the height above sea level, under standard air conditions, at which a given airplane is unable to climb faster than 100 feet per minute) with pullout initiated at no higher than 10,000 feet and recovery to level flight no greater than 5,000 feet. There had been some discussion as to why the peak load factor was four mph slower than the maximum speed attained on the last 70-degree dive. Subsequently, a Navy lieutenant, who was an unrated engineering officer, seriously recommended that a 110-degree dive be performed so that the seven Gs could be attained at the 90 degree attitude while the aircraft was still accelerating.

He would not back off from this requirement until theoretical dive profiles were carefully examined at Douglas' engineering department at El Segundo. These proved that a *lower* IAS would be attained because pullout would have to be initiated at a higher altitude of 12,000 feet for a safe recovery.

My next time out, I started the 90-degree dive from a service ceiling of about 30,000 feet using normal-rated power on the engine and the zero G pushover technique.

An extended vertical dive requires the ultimate in concentration by the test pilot. During the zero G pushover my eyes danced between the G meter, attitude gyro and oil pressure gauge. I held the G meter as close to zero G as possible during the pushover to 90 degrees attitude, to obtain zero lift and to reduce the drag, and I monitored the attitude gyro to be sure that the vertical attitude was not exceeded. And I repeatedly checked the oil pressure gauge to ensure the engine was getting proper lubrication.

During the vertical part of the dive I scanned the attitude gyro and altimeter primarily, with occasional glances at the airspeed, oil pressure, rpm, and turn and bank instruments. I needed the attitude gyro to be sure I was holding the 90-degree dive, and the altimeter (which was unwinding at a rate of slightly less than 1,000 feet per second) to make sure I started the pullout at 10,000 feet. The airspeed indicator advised me if the aircraft was about to exceed maximum design speed, while the oil pressure reading again indicated sufficient engine lubrication. The rpm gauge would tell me if I was over speeding the engine and the turn and bank indicator assured I was not in a skid, which would slow the airplane. The directional gyro, cylinder head and oil temperature gauges, and rate of descent indicator, were of no interest in this maneuver. I wasn't going anywhere except straight down. The temperatures would only be decreasing because of the increased airspeed. The rate of descent meter would be pegged.

As the altimeter needle swept through 10,000 feet I began the pullout and immediately sensed that something was wrong. Even though I was exerting a strong pull on the stick, I could not attain more than 2.3 Gs! Even with both hands applying a 200 pound pull-force on the stick, I could only gain another .2 g. (Incidentally, the 200 pound stick force was the design limit on the control system.) The ground was coming at me fast, but the pullout was gradually occurring. I didn't have any thoughts at the time that I wasn't going to make it. Yet I was very relieved as the nose of the Skyraider rose mightily up through the horizon. I had bottomed out at 2,200 feet.

I was very shaken. This was far too close for comfort. Further, because of the rapid pressure change, my ears hurt like hell.

Thinking about it, I could have taken one hand off the stick, opened the speed brakes and retarded the throttle for the recovery. But I am glad I didn't because this would have nullified the dive demonstration. I would have had to repeat the flight all over.

Returning to the air station after the dive, I wondered why there was such a vast difference in the pullout characteristics of the airplane compared to the previous flight. I also wondered how close I came to "buying the farm," the airman's traditional term for a fatal ground auguring crash.

My Navy chase pilot didn't help matters during the flight back when he commented over the radio that he had picked out the spot where I was going to bore a big hole in the Maryland countryside. My ears were pretty much plugged for several days from diving nearly 28,000 feet to a relatively low altitude while in a 90 degree attitude most of the way down. I later figured out that my maximum rate of descent was 44,000 feet per minute, quite a contrast from an unpressurized airliner descending at 500 feet per minute

The speed at seven Gs was 488 mph with a maximum IAS of 493, only five mph faster than with the 70-degree dive. It was not the 90-degree dive angle that produced the higher speed, but the *lower* recovery altitude. The IAS of the dive profiles in both the 70 and 90-degree dives prior to pullout were essentially the same because the airplane had reached terminal velocity due to the high drag rise.

This was my first encounter with the dreaded compressibility in any airplane. Compressibility, as it applies to aeronautics, is that portion of the airstream which is going past the airframe at the speed of sound, caused mainly by the shape of the leading edge of the wing. I had heard the term before, but it was a phenomenon that always happened to somebody else, people who dive sleek fighters toward the earth, not thick-winged attack bombers.

The reason I did not detect the compressibility in the 70-degree dive was because I initiated pullout at 8,000 feet, at which altitude the Mach number (Mach One is the speed of sound) of .74 had decayed from its maximum of .75. The reason for the greater loss in altitude for recovery from the 90-degree profile was only partially due to the increased dive angle. The prime cause was the effect of compressibility at 10,000 feet at .75 Mach, attesting to the impact of the seemingly minor but altogether significant difference between .74 and .75 Mach airspeed which allowed only 2.5 Gs with maximum pilot effort until the Mach No. decayed to a lower value. Mach .75 was the critical Mach number on the AD-1, which means that a shock wave has occurred which affects control of the airplane.

I was disappointed at being unable to hit the design speed of 500 mph but had tried my best. I made a total of nine dives, including build-up tests, using different entry techniques, dive angles and pullout altitudes, but we still fell seven mph short.

In the real world, the design speed maximum is one of the key characteristics a fighter or an attack airplane can have. Reason? It frees the service pilot from any concern about exceeding a red-line speed. Simply put, the airplane was designed for a higher speed than can be physically attained.

In retrospect, I have often wondered what "might have been" if the electrical stabilizer had been used for recovery, or if the 110-degree dive had been performed. In the latter case, boring a hole in the ground seemed to me the likely result, in which case someone else would be telling this story. Kermit Van Every, the chief aerodynamicist at Douglas, verified this thought when he told me at a Douglas retiree luncheon in 1992, "From what we know now, if the dive had been made at 110 degrees, you wouldn't have made it."

Another test point on the Vn diagram is the PHAA – plus high angle of attack. This involved the left-hand side of the diagram. My first attempt to demonstrate that portion of the Skyraider's Vn chart at 295 mph resulted in only 6.6 Gs during the pullout instead of the required 7. This was unacceptable to the Navy, not only because I didn't get 7 G but because execution of full aft stick deflection required an excessive length of time: .8 second. The requirement was .5 second.

Initially, I thought it was ridiculous to maneuver an airplane in such a manner. I intended to object to the requirement. But then I recalled a scenario on a fighter mission during the war when I *heard* an enemy aircraft's machine gun firing before I saw his aircraft. I looked around at my six o'clock position and found a Focke-Wulf 190 with the biggest radial engine I ever saw, not more than 100 feet away.

Oddly, and luckily for me, he didn't hit me with his guns. I reasoned that since guns are boresighted to converge at a point to provide maximum damage on impact, the 190's bullets must have been bracketing on both sides of my fuselage and converging in the distance ahead of me. I could actually hear his guns firing. Had he scored a hit he might have been in trouble for the debris from my Spit would probably have destroyed his bird.

Anyway, I broke right so violently in the Spitfire that I went into an accelerated stall and spun out. To my amazement, when I recovered from the spin, I was on the Jerry's tail in a steep dive. I chased him for awhile, but since I had just recovered from a spin and he was already at max speed, I had no chance of catching him.

This combination of defensive/offensive maneuver was never documented for evaluation, but perhaps it should have been. In the late 1980s the pilot of a Soviet Su27 fighter at the Paris Air Show performed the "Cobra" maneuver, a defensive/offensive maneuver during which he abruptly pulls up, which rapidly slows the airplane in order to force a pursuing adversary to whiz past him, then accelerates in for the kill.

The point is, a violent maneuver is sometimes required as a fraction of a second can occasionally be the difference between getting shot down or escaping from a pursuer.

I finally accepted the requirement for full aft stick deflection in one-half of a second. But that led to a dilemma encountered on the next flight. At the designated speed of 295 mph in level flight I grasped the stick with both hands and pulled back as sharply as I could to execute the pull-up. I reduced the time to only .6 seconds, registering 6.7 Gs on the airframe. I got no sympathy from Pax flight test personnel because they told me a Martin Aircraft Company test pilot in an AM Marauder had, indeed, achieved the magic number of .5 seconds.

Believing that I, too, possessed sufficient strength, or "the right stuff," I took this as a challenge. If a Marauder pilot could do it, so could I. I could lift weights to increase arm strength. On the other hand, a less time-consuming endeavor would be to use the technique of pre-trimming the airplane with a 20-pound *push* force (meaning nose-up trim and pushing against the stick in level flight) and yanking full aft on the stick with both hands. This pre-trimmed flight condition is not realistic for routine flight, but the main purpose at the time was to please the customer by hitting the left hand corner of the Vn diagram.

On the next flight I tried this technique and it worked. I achieved full elevator deflection in .48 seconds and increased the G load to a more acceptable 6.8.

All of the PHAA maneuvers resulted in violent buffet, severe shudder, and a dangerous high-pitch attitude of about 70 degrees. In addition, post-flight inspection of the Skyraider revealed that the fuel cell had broken away from its mounts and was dangerously close to pinching the hose that fed fuel to the engine.

It wasn't the reduction of .12 seconds for full elevator deflection that caused the .1 G increase. Rather, it was the change to a more nose-down leading edge stabilizer (from the pre-trimming) that resulted in more elevator control power, i.e. more down load on the tail.

I received a $5,000 risk bonus for the aerodynamic and structural tests and spins in the XBT2D/AD, the largest single amount I had ever received. I was so impressed by such a vast sum that I actually held onto the check for several weeks before cashing it, retrieving it now and then from a desk drawer, just to stare at it.

Considering a 1946 Buick convertible, which I purchased to replace my 1940 automobile, cost $2,600 in those days, that $5,000 was no small amount of money.

In my free time at Pax I had permission to check out in the Navy's F6F, F7F, F4U and F8F fighters. I also flew the F2G, a Goodyear-built version of the famed Chance Vought F4U Corsair. The company was especially interested in my evaluation of the F2G because Douglas was considering installing the same R-4360 "corn cob" engine in the Skyraider. Company engineers were particularly concerned about directional control on take-off with all of that additional horsepower, 3,500.

Fifteen minutes after take-off in the F2G one afternoon, I was in level flight at 3,000 feet en route to the assigned test area. I was getting acquainted with the airframe and was impressed with the aircraft's excellent level flight airspeed.

Suddenly, I was startled to see a twin-engine Navy JRB at my altitude and at my ten o'clock position. We were so close I saw the look of absolute horror on the face of the copilot. I tried to push over, down and away to avoid a collision, but it was too late. The horrid sound of metal striking metal with untold force filled my ears. The JRB had slammed into the aft portion of the Corsair. The props of the JRB tore off the entire tail section of my aircraft. In an instant I was tumbling recklessly in the sky. The stricken JRB was also out of control plummeting toward the ground.

I blew the canopy off in preparation for bailout. The wind whipped furiously around me, and the ground was coming up fast. I tried to raise up twice from the seat but couldn't. I was now at 1,000 feet, desperate, when I noticed that I had not unfastened my safety belt. "Dumb sumbitch!" I shouted to myself.

I released the belt and straight-away popped out of the Corsair with no time to spare. The chute blossomed several hundred feet above the ground and got tangled in a tree as I plunged through it, softening my impact with the ground. I landed in a field near highway 235 in Maryland and was scratched badly about the arms and face from the tree branches but was otherwise OK. Tragically, the two Naval officers and two civilians in the JRB, returning to their jobs at the Navy's Bureau of Aeronautics in Washington, were killed.

When I got back to the base I tried to call the Douglas Company in Santa Monica but couldn't get through to anyone in authority.

Obviously, I had something important to tell them, having been in a mid-air collision where lives had been lost. After several more attempts Bob Brush's secretary told me that Russ Thaw, George Jansen and two crew members had bailed out of a C-74 cargo plane. That was a double blow for Douglas, one bailout on the East coast and one on the West coast at precisely the same time. The odds of that ever happening must be astronomical.

In the aftermath of this awful tragedy, there was litigation by survivors of the JRB personnel. I was faulted by the civilian judge who was either unfamiliar with the right-of-way rules of the sky or didn't respect them. He claimed that since my aircraft was smaller than the JRB, it was my responsibility to avoid the larger plane. Giving way to the right was, and remains, a standard procedure for aircraft in the sky and boats on water. Since I was on the right of the JRB, my reasoning opposed that of the judge. But we, Douglas and I, lost the case.

Perhaps the toughest task I ever faced in my life was writing letters to the survivors of the men lost in the JRB, expressing my condolences and explaining how the accident happened, since I was the only witness. In retrospect, Old Man Fate had to have been in my corner again that day. Had the JRB been a split second faster or my Corsair a split second slower, the JRB's props would have struck my cockpit, instead of the empennage, and wiped me out as well.

After two emergency bailouts and one wheels-up forced landing in less than a year with Douglas, my boss, Bob Brush, felt that an assignment to less hazardous testing would be appropriate. So I was tasked with a *simple* program entailing a level flight, low altitude, emergency power water injection, engine cooling test.

On September 27, 1946, I was tooling along in a Skyraider, pulling sixty-one inches of manifold pressure on the R-3350 engine just off shore near Manhattan Beach. I was enjoying the scenery when all of a sudden the engine caught fire. "I just can't bail out three times in one year!" I thought. Alternate landing sites ran through my mind: Torrance Airport, Hughes Airport, LAX, the beach, or I could belly into the ocean. Torrance was behind me which meant a time-consuming, risky 180-degree turn; Hughes was too far away; and if I could help it, I didn't want to damage the plane landing on the beach at El Segundo or the ocean.

So I decided to "dead stick" the Skyraider into Los Angeles International Airport. Unfortunately, the radio had failed, so contact with the company or the control tower at LAX to inform them of the emergency was impossible.

At low altitude I could not make a standard pattern, so I flew an improvised approach toward the field, diagonal to the runway, which helped me see it, since smoke was billowing from the engine. I maneuvered so that I could land downwind but lacking communication with the tower, I had no knowledge of incoming traffic. I had my eyes fixed on the *other*, or approach, end of the runway, looking for normal landing traffic. If somebody else was trying to land – opposite to my approach – I planned to put the aircraft down on the grass adjacent to the airstrip.

In any case, I touched down and after 500 feet of roll-out on the concrete, I hit right brake and rolled across the infield grass and the taxi strip right up to within 100 feet of the fire station on the south side of the airport.

To this day, I believe that, due to the radio failure, people in the control tower, located on the north side of the field, never knew about the Skyraider which made an emergency landing on their airport. There was no summons from the controllers asking, "Please telephone the tower and explain your actions." I had been on the runway for only a few seconds. Needless to say, the fire fighters were quite surprised to discover a smoking airplane parked directly in front of their ramp and rapidly contained the conflagration.

Forty-six years later I was on a bus traveling to Point Mugu, California for a tour of the naval base there, sponsored by the Society of Experimental Test Pilots. I sat beside a man I had not met before. He was a former mechanic on the P-82 at North American, whose flight ramp was adjacent to Douglas Aircraft's. I told him that a P-82 pilot probably saved my life when he found me out in the ocean after I bailed out from the nose-less BT2D some time earlier.

The man told me of a Douglas incident that he had witnessed involving a Skyraider that was on fire and smoking badly at it landed downwind at LAX. He remembered that the pilot exited the plane hurriedly after it had come to a stop. I told him that I was that swift pilot. Small world.

It was after this incident that I began to seriously question whether I should continue in this line of endeavor. Assessing the events of the past year of my working life: I had crash-landed a P-47 in the trees in Ohio, bellied in a Skyraider at Patuxent River, dead-sticked an AD into LAX and had two petrifying bailouts – one when the front end of my BT2D flew off the airplane, and one when the rear of the F2G was sliced off by the JRB.

Maybe now was the time to pursue less hazardous goals, becoming an airline pilot, or rejoining the Air Force, even though the service was releasing aviators by the thousands.

I talked with Bob Brush and Eric Springer, Donald Douglas' very first test pilot, who was serving as Vice President and General Manager of the El Segundo plant. These were soul-searching discussions. Brush and Springer agreed that the dangers of test flying were indeed considerable, and that I had surely had far more than my fair share of misadventures in the sky. Neither Springer nor Brush tried to persuade me one way or the other, but they did subtly suggest that matters like this eventually evened out, that the future was bound to get better – and safer – for me. I decided to stick with Douglas for awhile and see what happened.

As a gesture of reprieve, Brush pulled me from the regular flight test schedule. Subsequently, I flew the company C-47 on routine trips to Douglas' missile base in White Sands, New Mexico and other locations.

On one trip I was late arriving at the aircraft which was already filled with engineers en route to Naval Air Station Moffett Field near San Francisco. The pilot was already in the left seat. I clambered aboard wearing my customary back-pack parachute out of habit. In order to reach the cockpit I had to walk from the fuselage door at the rear through the aisle between the rows of passenger seats. Once in the cockpit I methodically began strapping in the seat.

"Where's your chute?" I asked the pilot.

"Parachute?" he asked, incredulous.

It then dawned on me that I was the only individual on the aircraft *with* a parachute. I squirmed in my seat, embarrassed beyond imagination. Five years of flying single-engine aircraft, where a parachute was as much a part of my equipment as a radio mike, had conditioned me. I became the butt of a thousand jokes that day.

After a time I returned to the Skyraider flight test schedule. A backlog of planes was ready for test at the same time so one of my flights was reassigned to fellow test pilot, Jack Armstrong. Jack was primarily a transport or cargo plane test pilot but he had checked out in the AD. His job that day was to *stress test* the Aeroproducts propeller.

He was airborne in the test area off the coast when, with a loud bang, all four propeller blades spun off the Skyraider. The attack bomber instantly became a glider. It was later discovered than an O ring seal had been installed improperly, allowing oil to escape from the prop housing. Jack's recount of the accident contained the phrase, "Thank heaven all the blades left simultaneously." If they hadn't, he might have ended up in the drink like I did when the bomb hit the prop.

Armstrong decided to dead-stick it into Santa Monica Airport. This was a challenge because both the approach and landing ends of the runway were elevated. Undershoot and you might slam into the bank. Overshoot, and you could plow into houses situated off the end of the runway.

46

Jack hit the airstrip about mid-field with excess speed, went off the end, crashed into a street at the perimeter of the field and bounced smack into the roof of a house. In the process the engine came off, struck the windshield and grazed the top of Jack's head. He was trapped in the aircraft for awhile before being freed. He survived but in addition to a concussion, scrapes and bruises, broke his leg and ankle.

His was an extremely difficult landing to make, not only because of the elevated runway, but because the loss of the prop blades made the airplane light. Further, and more importantly, drag was sharply reduced since there was no windmilling propeller up front.

There is no way to practice landing in such a configuration. Douglas rebuilt the damaged home and for many years it was referred to in our circles as, "The House That Jack Built."

I sympathized with Jack for what happened on a flight which normally would have been mine. At the same time, this event led me to believe that maybe my luck was changing. Misfortune was busy elsewhere.

Young Bob Rahn (left) with his brother Ivan look on as their father works on the family's 1923 Studebaker.

Bob poses (second from left) with his first airplane, a Luscombe.

A Bell P-39 Airacobra of the 31st Fighter Group. (Bell Aircraft Corp.)

Pilots of the 309th Fighter Sq. at Chichester, England in July 1942. Bob Rahn is third from the left. The officer third from the right is 31st Group CO, Col. John R. Hawkins. (Signal Corps)

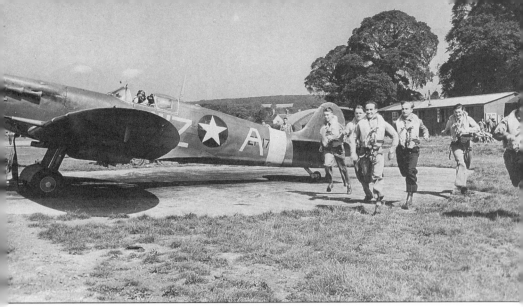

Scrambling to their Spit Vs in England are pilots of the 309th Fighter Sq. CO, Harry Thyng is in the cockpit and Bob Rahn is the joyous youth on the far right. (Signal Corps)

Bob Rahn, face bandaged, leans against the remains of his Spitfire, demolished during a take-off scramble in North Africa. The other aircraft are French.

A B-17 Flying Fortress of the type employed in RAZON tests from Wendover, Utah. Bob Rahn was piloting one when a fire broke out. Because one crew member could not bail out Bob stayed with the badly damaged plane and landed it.

Members of the second AF Test Pilot Training School class at Wright-Patterson, (l. to r.) Captains Don Gentile (famed VIII AF ace), Bob Rahn and Chilstrom (first AF pilot to fly the F-86 jet). (USAF)

One of Rahn's
early test
assignments was
with the Bell P-59,
the first jet fighter

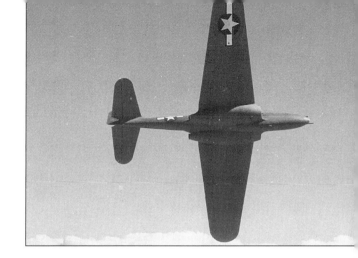

A late model North
American P-51H
Mustang.

Maj. Dick Bong, who scored 40 aerial victories in the Lockheed P-38 Lightning (like the one
shown here) in Pacific combat, was one of the Wright Field test pilots who dueled Rahn in
mock dog fights.

This series of three photos shows the battered remains of a Republic P-47N that Bob Rahn landed on an Ohio farm, after engine failure.

1945 vintage Douglas test pilots. Top row: (l. to r.) Jansen, Browne, unknown and Morrisey. Seated: Rahn, Martin, Brush and Thaw (Douglas)

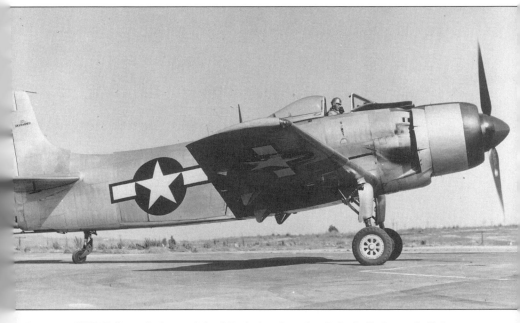

Prototype XBT2D (later designated the AD-1), the plane that Rahn bailed out of off the California coast. (McDonnell Douglas)

Wearing an anti-G suit, Rahn mounts an AD-1. (McDonnell Douglas, Harry Gann)

Remains of the AD-1 that Rahn bellied in near Pax River NAS.

Remains of the F2G Corsair flown by Rahn that was involved in a mid-air collision over Maryland. (USN)

The Douglas AD-1 Skyraider was loaded with 10,000 lbs. of external stores at take-off for an unofficial single-engine world record.

The AD-3W "Guppy" test flown by Rahn. The belly mounted radome separated during a high speed pullout. Rahn was advised by radio, "You lost your boat." (Mc Donnell Douglas, Harry Gann)

The XA2D turboprop and test pilot George Jansen. (Mc Donnell Douglas, Harry Gann)

The Douglas DC-6 transport in which Rahn tested for carbon dioxide gases released by actuating fire extinguishers. (McDonnell Douglas)

The Douglas F3D-1 Skyknight, the "Pussycat" beloved by Rahn, scored the first night jet-to-jet aerial victory of the Korean War. (Mc Donnell Douglas, Harry Gann)

A first jet flight for the media was made in the Skyknight. (l. to r.) Don Durggin, LA Daily News; unknown Navy officer; Julian Hartt, LA Examiner; Bob Rahn; Clete Roberts, CBS TV news; and Marvin Miles, LA Times. (Mc Donnell Douglas)

The Douglas XF4D Skyray in 1951 with a 5,000 lb thrust J-35 engine. (Mc Donnell Douglas)

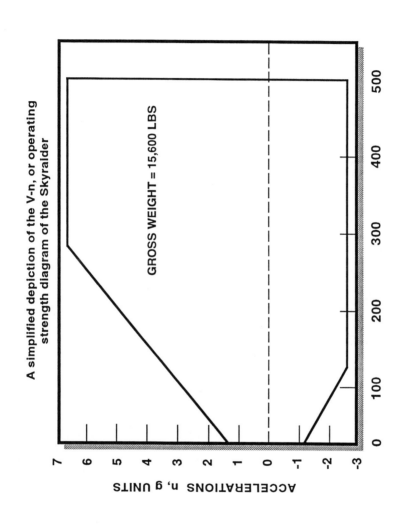

A simplified depiction of the V-n, or operating strength diagram of the Skyralder

GROSS WEIGHT = 15,600 LBS

The Navy's first preliminary evaluation team for the Skyray: (l. to r.) Bob Rahn, Marion Carl (an 18.5 victory Marine ace of WW II), Bob Clark and Bob Elder. (McDonnell Douglas)

The Douglas XF4D-1 Skyray equipped with a J-40 engine, in the racer configuration. (Mc Donnell Douglas)

A Skyray produces a shock wave during a high speed pass over Edwards AFB. (Mc Donnell Douglas)

Douglas engineers getting together with Lt. Cdr. Jim Verdin (in flight suit) for a pre speed trial technical conference. Bob Rahn said, "Notice that I am the one who is chewing his nails."

Rahn congratulates Verdin on completion of the 3 km speed record, Oct 3, 1953. (Mc Donnell Douglas)

Rahn taxis out for the 100 km closed course record try, Oct 16, 1953.

5

MORE ON THE SKYRAIDER

Shortly after World War II the B-36 bomber "weenies" of the Air Force were lording it over the fighter jocks because they claimed they could fly higher than the fighters and therefore, could not be intercepted. In those days very few propeller planes could make their way to 40,000 feet. For some of us with the capability, however, it became a popular pastime to fly to this exalted height to prove that you were flying the latest and best equipment.

This was not awfully difficult for the AD. We took a *standard* production plane and filled it with only 100 gallons of fuel. We did *forget* to install the guns, ammunition, wing racks and missiles, however. I climbed to a service ceiling of a little over 39,000 feet, but experienced some very painful bends in my left wrist in the process. This rendered my left hand useless.

I achieved the desired altitude by slowly climbing to 40,610 feet, which proved to be the absolute ceiling of the AD. We realized this was an insignificant achievement because we didn't have an effective weapon on board. Besides, the Skyraider stalled and the engine quit. I worked the throttle with my able right hand as I tried to restart the engine and flew the aircraft with my knees on the stick. On the way down I got the engine going again and landed safely but with only ten gallons of fuel remaining.

The effort did demonstrate the importance of weight in relation to climbing performance. I had achieved an altitude 10,000 feet higher than thought possible in the standard configuration of the aircraft.

I made one flight in the basic AD at maximum gross weight at LAX with 10,000 pounds of bombs on the external racks for stability and control purposes. The aircraft passed all checks, but was marginal in roll rate in the power approach (PA) configuration. Also, speed acceleration in the approach was less than impressive. I made a long, straight-in approach with high power and low sink rate to land safely.

The flight was heralded as a significant accomplishment because the Skyraider carried more ordnance than either the B-17 or B-24, World War II heavies. The feat was an unofficial record. In 1954, however, at Naval Air Station Dallas, the Navy scored an official world record when a Skyraider took off with 10,500 pounds of ordnance on board.

There were seven models of the Skyraider built, with a multitude of versions over the years, testimony to the value of the design concepts of Ed Heinemann and his team of engineers. Fundamental simplicity was the key and it paid huge dividends in the AD, which was a workhorse in two wars and for a long time existed on flight decks along with its faster, jet-powered brothers. I won't go into all the various models and versions here but will comment on the AD-3W because I spent a lot of time flying it.

The main difference between the AD-3W, commonly known as the "Guppy," and the basic AD was the large radome slung underneath the fuselage. The radome was about eight by twelve by three feet deep and housed radar for early warning missions. Unlike the *straight* Skyraider, the Guppy had fuel tanks in the wing but neither armament nor dive brakes. It accommodated two radar operators who sat in the aft fuselage where the fuel tank was on the basic model.

When the designers try to add something to any airplane, the basic characteristics are usually adversely affected. Directional stability was notably diminished in the AD-3W over the basic AD because of the large radome – rudder lock occurred during sideslips. (Sideslip flight was a test requirement.) Two vertical fins were added to the horizontal stabilizer which eliminated the problem.

Full rudder pedal deflection on the AD-3W produced double the sideslip angle with only about one-half the pedal force (150 pounds versus 300 pounds in the basic airplane).

The cockpit environment was uncomfortable to me since full cross controls (rudder and opposite aileron) were required to hold the aircraft in a steady sideslip. A 45-degree dive angle was needed to hold speed due to increased drag from the high yaw angle and the relatively "dirty" configuration of the Guppy with its radome. The maximum allowable sideslip not only created maximum design loads on the tail but wedged me against the side of the cockpit.

Throughout the work-up flights and the final test, I couldn't rid my mind of the memory that Jack Armstrong lost a propeller doing prop load tests by yawing an AD. The yaw angles I was obtaining were twice what Jack was achieving during his accident.

The stall characteristics of the Guppy were immensely affected by the radome. In the landing configuration, the left wing dropped about 45 degrees at the stall point, whereas using normal-rated power, in the power approach configuration, the airplane abruptly rolled about 90 degrees at the stall, an unsatisfactory circumstance. Stall strips and outboard wing slats, helped correct this at the cost of cruise speed.

In earlier days Navy pilots came aboard a carrier with the canopy open to expedite evacuation in the event of an emergency. Therefore I conducted stall tests with the canopy open. During recovery from one stall, I pushed the stick forward abruptly to determine minimum loss of altitude for recovery. Suddenly, I found myself floating half-way out of the cockpit. I was able to pull myself back in with both hands on the stick. Somehow, my seat belt had become unfastened – probably caught by a sleeve. I would have had one heck of a time trying to explain why I bailed out of an airplane while conducting a simple stall test.

Later, in a dive in the AD-3W, I experienced mild buffet at maximum speed. During the pullout, as I approached the design load factor of 7 Gs, I felt a thud. The Skyraider pitched up abruptly at 9.3 Gs! The radome had separated from the aircraft. I instantly released back pressure on the stick and luckily avoided blacking out because I was wearing a G-suit.

"What else has departed the aircraft?" I asked myself. This was of concern because the 9.3 Gs exceeded by 33 percent the design load factor.

Plus, I was only 1.2 G below the point where the wings would have failed. There was no chase plane to advise me so I motored back to home base very carefully, as if I were in a jalopy limping to the nearest service station.

In the traffic pattern at Santa Monica the tower operator exclaimed, "You have lost your boat," referring to the radome. If that's all that was missing I was in comparatively good shape. Sure enough, after landing, we discovered only a few loose rivets in the wing, in addition to the missing radome. Upon closer inspection, though, there was a permanent bend in the wing spar. The Guppy had to be scratched from the inventory.

Contemplating this incident, I felt a new measure of respect for the AD. It had held together under severe circumstances. Whenever I heard the adjective "rugged" applied to the Skyraider I felt it perfectly appropriate.

When it came to spins, the AD-1 and the AD-3W were like Dr. Jekyll and Mr. Hyde. There was an assortment of avionics boxes and two crew members in the rear fuselage of the early warning model, which shifted the center of gravity (CG) aft. The radome diminished directional stability to such an extent that spin characteristics were flat with the rudder locked over. On the company radio frequency I described the unnerving characteristics of the spin I was experiencing. The control column was ineffective as I wound down toward the ground. In my frustration I declared, "You can throw the stick out the cockpit for all its worth!" Fortunately, foresight predicted the need for a spin chute in such an emergency. Now was the time to use it.

As I was whirling down – in a flat spin, as it turned out – I actuated the spin chute. It didn't perform as advertised and chase pilot, Jim Seay suggested I bail out, but the unopened chute did produce a downward pitching moment which got me out of the flat spin and enabled me to use conventional techniques to recover. Whew!

Jim, incidentally, was later killed in an AD-5 at Patuxent while performing a negative G pushover maneuver.

I was delivering an AD-3N (N represented night operations) to Pax when my mother died. I had a stopover at Knoxville, Tennessee and company officials were unable to reach me, and I learned about her passing at Patuxent River next day. She was taken by cancer at the relatively young age of 54. That caution she gave me when I went off to join the Air Corps in 1941, "Fly low and slow," was aerodynamically flawed, but in human terms, one of the great memories of my life.

There were 3,180 Skyraiders in seven models and many versions built over a period of 12 years. It had earned a couple additional nicknames beyond those mentioned in the previous chapter, "Old Faithful" and "Able Dog," for instance. They all fit. It was one of the best flying machines ever built.

6

THE SKYSHARK –
NOT FOR ME, PLEASE

From 1945 through 1949, the Skyraider occupied most of my professional life, but I did make occasional test flights as copilot in the Super DC-3, C-74, C-124, DC-4 and DC-6.

In the case of the last, we were trying to determine what happened on the DC-6 which crashed in 1948 killing all on board including the famous showman, Earl Carroll. The initial investigation revealed that the crew had been asphyxiated by carbon dioxide gases which flooded into the cockpit after the fire-extinguishing bottles had been actuated to put out a fire in the baggage compartment.

In order to test this theory, we went aloft wearing cumbersome gas masks in the cockpit while we conducted contamination tests of the surrounding air in the cockpit. We initiated an emergency descent by lowering the gear, pushing over to negative g, retarding the throttles to idle, and depressurizing the cabin and baggage compartment This confirmed that carbon dioxide gases had indeed wafted up to the cockpit and caused the tragedy. It proved to be a weird experience flying a modern commercial transport while wearing full face gas masks.

Meanwhile, I had thoroughly enjoyed the bachelor life but at 27, in 1948, it ultimately dawned on me that it might be a good idea to settle down. I had long since concluded that test flying was more hazardous than combat flying. In experimental test work it was absolutely essential that I be ahead of the airplane at all times. I had to be able to analyze a problem and make an immediate decision to correct it. A split second could spell the difference between life and death.

I had met Jane Shumway, an utterly lovely lady, in Douglas' Washington D.C. office during a trip to the nation's capital in 1946 when I was doing test work at Patuxent River. We were attracted to each other, and eventually Jane transferred to California where she got a job at Douglas' Santa Monica plant. Our romance flourished and we were married in 1948 in the Little Church of the West in Las Vegas.

I assumed more regular hours and enjoyed being a family man. We had two children, a boy, Kenneth, and a girl, Sherry. I am convinced that I became a safer pilot in the air, not because I was trying harder, but because I was in better physical and mental state to do the job. I quickly gained 15 pounds, however, due to good cooking and the stable routine of married life.

We lived in Westwood where the final approach to the Santa Monica airport was a half block from my front door. If I had a late afternoon flight, as I neared the runway for landing, I glanced in the direction of our house. If Jane was standing on the front porch, I knew that dinner was ready and that I needed to hasten my post-flight report and get on home. On Saturdays, if I had to fly, I was allowed to stay home and do chores around the house, awaiting a summons to come to work. When the flight office had the necessary papers in order, indicating my airplane was preflighted and ready to go, Jerry Pearson, the flight dispatcher, hailed me via the public address system, which I could easily hear. I was in the cockpit within minutes. That's convenience.

After a time we moved to a bigger place in Bel Air, still not far from Santa Monica, however I soon began working full-time at Edwards Air Force Base in the desert where I normally stayed during the week, hustling home on weekends.

By 1949 the only other new fighter or light attack aircraft on the flight line at Douglas was the XF3D jet, which test pilot Russ Thaw was putting through its paces. I asked Bob Brush if I could get into that program, since I had flown the P-59 and P-80 jets, but it couldn't be done. I was disappointed and also felt slighted and a little angry because when I had joined Douglas in 1945, I was the only pilot in the company who had flown a jet and thought that experience should have worked in my favor.

Meanwhile, North American Aviation, just across the street from the Douglas El Segundo plant, was flight testing its new heavy attack bomber, the AJ Savage. I made some feelers and decided to apply for a job on the Savage at this competing company. Although I was turned down, I wasn't terribly hurt because I realized that, in my heart, I wouldn't like testing such large airplanes.

In the end, my rejection was a blessing in disguise. The pilot hired instead of me was subsequently killed during a high-speed yaw test in the AJ. The tail of the Savage tore off the bomber, which went out of control and crashed.

There's that mysterious phenomenon, Fate, again.

I considered this accident and Jack Armstrong's and reasoned that maybe my luck really was changing. Maybe I ought to stay right where I was and continue flying for Douglas.

Not long after this, Bob Brush called me into his office. "How would you like to fly the XA2D?" he asked.

"I'd love it!" I answered, without hesitation.

Brush said, "We've assigned George Jansen to make the first flight and the engine/propeller developmental flights. But we'd like you to fly the aerodynamic and structure demos plus the spin tests."

"I'm your man," I said, enthusiastically.

The Skyshark represented an innovative step forward in aviation technology. It was the United States' first postwar tactical aircraft driven by a turboprop (propeller and compressor driven by a jet turbine power plant). It featured counter-rotating propellers geared to two gas turbines, had a fuselage very similar to the Skyraider's, was designed for long range bombing runs and would cruise at over 300 knots in level flight. The counter rotating props were necessary to restrain the torque on take-off because the Allison T-40-A engine developed over 5,000 horsepower.

The Skyshark's first flight was delayed because the engine failed a qualifying 50-hour run on the test stand. The gear box and prop controls were other dilemmas. George finally went aloft in the Skyshark in May 1950 and performed some rudimentary developmental work required for the Naval Preliminary Evaluation (NPE). He had all kinds of problems with the airplane, but by December it was deemed satisfactory for an NPE.

In the meantime I was assigned to perform the structural and aerodynamic demonstration and spins on the first production airplane of the F3D Skyknight series. Offered the opportunity to fly the Skyshark prior to the NPE, to obtain a second "company pilot" evaluation of the aircraft, I politely refused, explaining that I felt this would only further delay the XA2D program. Truth was, I had doubts about the plane, and my gut instinct was telling me to steer clear of it.

During the NPE of the Skyshark, Major – later Major General – Marion Carl, one of the Marine Corps' greatest heroes and pilots, made his first evaluation flight in the Skyshark at Edwards Air Force Base. He landed, taxied back to the ramp and parked the machine, but the counter-rotating propellers kept turning over and over and over. The engine, by the way, was noisier than hell. I was watching with some others and we began to wonder what Marion was doing because the props just kept spinning and spinning. At least five minutes, maybe ten, went by. The whining noise was high pitched and almost unbearable. We covered our ears with our hands against the sound.

Finally, after what seemed an eternity, Carl transmitted over the radio on the test frequency. "How do you shut this damn thing down?"

We gave him the necessary instructions, laughing like hell amongst ourselves, and wouldn't let him forget his snafu for some time.

Lieutenant Commander Hugh Wood was killed in the airplane during the NPE. Subsequent investigation revealed that one of the power units had failed. Its compressor absorbed the complete power output from the remaining good engine, simultaneously extracting considerable energy from the prop. The props went to full low pitch (high rpm) which, with six wide blades whirling around, acted like the plane was pushing a barn door ahead of itself. With all this drag and little power the Skyshark came down at an excessive sink rate. Wood was unable to flare sufficiently to cushion his landing and slammed violently into the earth.

After literally years of engine/gear box/prop development problems, a new *production* engine was installed. The first flight took place in June 1953. Again I was asked if I wanted to fly the airplane, but by this time I had been assigned to the XF4D Skyray program and was greatly enthralled with the project. So I declined, stating that I had agreed to demonstrate the *airframe*, not the *power plant*.

Shortly thereafter, Gordon "Doc" Livingston, a former Navy pilot hired by Douglas, had one of the scariest rides of his life in the Skyshark. He was near Muroc Dry Lake when he lost the complete front end of the airplane which included the counter-rotating props and a major portion of the gear box. To maintain flight he had to hold in full forward stick. His chase pilot and engineers on the ground advised him to bail out.

"I think I can bring it in," he radioed back. The chase pilot and engineers were nervously skeptical. But in a crucial situation like this, the pilot at the controls calls the shots. This proved academic because it turned out he couldn't get the canopy to open far enough to bail out. He was obliged to stay with the headless monster.

The strain on Doc's mind and body in that approach, holding the control column full forward, dead-sticking all the way, with wheels down, was formidable indeed. Yet he managed to set the Skyshark down on the dry lake in one piece. Moreover, it didn't catch fire. Quite a feat of flying.

A little later, after Doc's hairy ride, George Jansen had to eject from one of the Skysharks with the so-called *production* engine installed, when the gear box failed. He sustained a serious back injury and was in a cast for months.

The Skyshark tally was not good: one death, one bailout, one extreme emergency landing (which should have been a bailout), and never ending propeller/gearbox/engine problems.

So, as time went by, and I was occasionally asked if I wanted to fly the XA2D, I had no qualms about replying, "No, thanks. Maybe later, after George develops it."

Normally, a test pilot wants to fly as many planes as he can. I believed I had as much courage as the next guy, but I had no second thoughts whatsoever about restricting the Skyshark. Indeed, the aircraft never went into production because of its insurmountable problems.

There was a meeting in Ed Heinemann's office about the turboprop and after lengthy discussion the Navy Project Officer asked Douglas officials what they thought about continuing the Skyshark. Ben Collins, the A2D Project Engineer, said, "We're just tired. We've had enough."

That was the death knell of the Skyshark program.

Once in awhile, nowadays, I visit the Chino Airport in California. Resting forlornly beside a hangar is the hulk of an A2D Skyshark but sans the engines. Invariably, I take a long look at the aircraft and say to myself, "I almost left the Douglas company because I was afraid I wouldn't get assigned to fly this aircraft." I never considered it a very pretty plane to begin with, but it did have an awesome look about it. Nonetheless, I have never regretted not flying it.

7

JET-PROPELLED PUSSY CAT

The F3D Skyknight night fighter, designed for the Navy, was a pussy cat, an old man's airplane. Powered by a pair of Westinghouse J-34-WE-24 engines producing 3,250 pounds of thrust each, it lacked great performance in terms of speed, but was easy to fly and quite comfortable, especially for cross country flights. An upgraded version (WE-36) of 3,400 pounds thrust came along later for the F3D-2.

The straight wing of 50-foot span was mounted on the mid-portion of the fuselage. Engines occupied the lower center portion of the fuselage. Its empennage was similar to the Douglas early jet driven experimental research plane, the D-558-1 Skystreak.

The Skyknight featured side by side seating for the pilot and radar operator. An escape chute – sometimes called the laundry chute – ran from aft of the cockpit to the bottom of the fuselage to facilitate bail-out in an emergency. The F3D's gross weight, with 1,174 gallons of fuel on board, located entirely in the fuselage, was 21,500 pounds. There were four 20 millimeter cannons mounted in the nose just ahead of the engine inlet ducts.

I was assigned to fly the aerodynamic, structural, and spin tests on the first F3D-1, Russ Thaw having made the maiden flight in the prototype XF3D in March 1948. I made my first flight on March 3, 1950, and liked the bird from the outset despite some problems and its lack of power. From the beginning, we had more difficulty developing the engine than we did the airplane itself because Russ had done such a good job on developing the control system.

Extreme care had to be exercised when starting the power plants, to prevent exceeding turbine outlet temperature (TOT) redline. Engine rpm was slow when accelerating from idle and vigilance was required not to exceed turbine red line temperatures. Turbine blade failures were not uncommon and when they failed they usually tore out through the side of the fuselage. Fortunately, none went inboard. Had they done so, they would have punctured the fuel tank or cut some of the control cables.

For those tests which were not considered *overly* hazardous, such as structural or aerodynamic demonstrations, or spins, we took a flight test engineer along. One accompanied me on a day when turbine blades ripped through the skin of the fuselage. I turned for home and started whistling.

"Bob, do you know that you always start whistling when you have an emergency?" the engineer said.

I had never noticed this tendency before and don't know when it started, but apparently it was a habit begun long before, perhaps even back to Spitfire days. (To this day, while flying my Navion when things become a bit *tight* due to bad weather or whatever, my wife claims I start whistling.) In my own mind I believe this habit possibly stems from that part of the psyche which inspires you to whistle when going through a graveyard at night, helping you gain, or regain, courage.

When firing the Skyknight's cannons, gases from the guns sometimes went down the air intakes causing engine flame-out, another serious problem. On one long test, flight engineer Bob Lafey brought along his "brown bag" lunch. We were out over San Clemente Island to fire the guns. After firing in a dive, it suddenly got *real quiet* in the cockpit of the F3D. Both engines had flamed out from the gun gases. I immediately commenced restart procedures as I pulled up from the dive trying to attain as much altitude as possible because San Clemente island was a long way from the mainland. While busily engaged with throttle and switches I noticed, through my peripheral vision, that Bob had unfastened his safety belt, grabbed his brown bag, was out of his seat, and was maneuvering toward the escape chute, about to hit the silk! With my right arm I reached out, grabbed him, and hauled him back into his seat. Then I continued the restart, getting both engines to light off in a reasonable amount of time.

After that, our heart rates subsided, and we flew back home. I never did ask Lafey if he intended to consume his lunch while floating down in his parachute or while bobbing in the ocean waiting for the rescue party. After only four flights, and four hours and twenty minutes in the Skyknight, I was surprised to be chosen to take Ed Heinemann up on his first ride in a jet, especially since Russ Thaw had over 100 hours and 100 flights in the XF3D.

Heinemann, of course, was *the* man at El Segundo, the chief engineer and a highly regarded designer of uncommon skill. His imprint was on many of Douglas' most successful tactical airplanes. We flew on a roll-rate test in the first production model of the Skyknight, Ed manning the radar operator seat.

"We'll be doing a lot of rolls, at varying speeds up to 500 miles per hour," I cautioned him.

"Don't let me interfere with any of your test programs. Just pretend I'm not there," he said sincerely.

"OK," I told him, "but please let me know if at any time you start to feel queasy."

Ed later wrote in his autobiography, "Bob wrung me and the airplane out thoroughly. Old man's aircraft that it was, in Rahn's hands it gave me a convincing taste of what jet-powered maneuverability is all about. I don't know how many times we whirled through the sky. Bob was right when he said afterwards that I was getting a bit green around the collar....Indeed, I consumed an entire package of gum while in the air."

The company newspaper, *Douglas Digest*, quoted Ed as noting the flight was as "smooth as a kitten's ear... smoothest flight I ever had." I wouldn't call doing a series of full stick deflection roll rate tests at numerous speeds as the smoothest flight I've ever had.

Four aviation writers from the Southern California area were given permission by Douglas and the Navy to ride in the jet, which was still considered new technology in the late 1940s and early 1950s. They were Don Dwiggins of the Los Angeles Daily News, Julian Hart of the Los Angeles Examiner, Clete Roberts of CBS-TV News, and Marvin Miles of the Los Angeles Times. Following are extracts from Marvin's account of our excursion in the brilliant blue, from the July 17, 1950 issue of the Los Angeles Times:

Twenty-two thousand pounds of high-speed baby buggy!...with radar eyes and a quadruple 20 mm voice! She was built for a highly specialized mission, searching out, tracking down, and destroying enemy aircraft at night, the Navy's first night fighter designed as such and her ceiling is above 40,000 feet.

Bundled in a yellow Mae West, parachute straps and a gold crash helmet, I climbed up the hand-and-foot holds on the fuselage and let myself down into the cockpit.

"First," said the 29 year old Douglas test pilot, "here's how we get out if we have to. See this red lever here? If I pull it, the seats swing back, this hatch on the floor opens – and another one at the bottom of the fuselage. Then you grab this vaulting bar, swing your feet into the tunnel and slide down and out the belly." Simple!

He went on explaining other gadgets in the cockpit, but I kept looking at the red lever and the hatch opening into a tunnel – a life-saving delivery chute into thousands of feet of space!

The two Westinghouse jets started with a roar. No fuss, no long cockpit check. Merely a quick – and deafening – full power run-up to check operations of the auxiliary fuel pump.

"Let's go," Rahn said.

After taxiing out to the runway he turned the ship into the wind at Los Angeles International Airport, paused briefly for tower clearance, then shoved the throttles full up.

The Skyknight gathered speed and more speed.

Rahn spoke over the intercom:

"She'll come unglued from the runway at about a hundred – and if you don't think she's sensitive, just watch."

He curled one finger around the stick and pulled back gently. The ship swept into the air as if she slid on greased rails.

Suddenly, white smoke filled the cockpit. I caught my breath, then exhaled, remembering the warning of Ed Heinemann, top Douglas engineer.

"There'll be 'smoke' in the cockpit when you're first airborne. It really isn't smoke, of course, but condensation from the plane's air conditioning system."

There was snow, too, tiny flakes of it that whirled about us in a miniature storm.

The Skyknight rode upward, reaching for altitude, while Rahn sat beside me, one finger on the stick, his eyes roving over the flickering needles on the instrument panel.

As we climbed, Rahn said, "We've got 100 (F3Ds) on order. She'll fly across country nonstop with 300 gallon wing tanks. The tanks can be used as napalm bombs or she'll lug two 2,000 pounders. She can cruise on one engine. Her radar is the most modern available. And she can see backward as well as forward."

He pushed the stick left and the ocean slid away from under us, coiled over the top of the cockpit and slid back into position again.

And another.

Again sea and sky played tag around us and the G-needle perked over to "two," registering my weight under two-fold gravity as 320 pounds.

(Later, Rahn said) "Now we'll try a stall."

Rahn dropped landing gear and flaps, let the Skyknight ride slower and slower until at last she shuddered almost imperceptibly and dipped her nose tiredly toward the sea.

"Beautiful isn't she, " the pilot beamed. "She was below 100 (mph) when she fell off. And I had lateral control right up to the last tick."

He fell silent after that. He seemed to be thinking. But he was fussing with cockpit gadgets, too.

"I'm sorry," he explained finally. "We'll have to go in. We've just lost our hydraulic pressure. The wheels wouldn't come up but half way. Got 'em down by gravity. They're locked and we're OK. Didn't want to tell you until I got things straightened out."

Calmly he outlined the next procedure:

"With our main hydraulics out, I'll have to use the aileron auxiliary to lower the flaps for landing. That gives me no boost for the ailerons so I'll have to use the stick extension to give me leverage against the straight air pressure."

He popped the extension up and we headed for home.

Everything was normal as far as I could see. Rahn handled the ship smoothly through a figure S, but he was using muscle now without help of hydraulic boost. He called the tower, reporting the hydraulic failure.

We slipped down the groove toward the runway, touched on the main wheels, rolled for several seconds, then the nose wheel settled.

"It's all in a day's work," the test pilot commented. "Little things that have to be corrected here and there. That's why I'm here."

When the red crash trucks raced out to meet us, he laughed.

"Sure didn't need 'em, but they're good insurance, I'd say."

Good aircraft....Good pilot – I'd say!

At one point we got behind schedule in the F3D preliminary demonstration tests at the plant and went to the municipal airport in Palm Springs, California, with three aircraft for exploratory and developmental tests prior to going to PAX for the final demonstration tests. In December 1950, at Palm Springs, the superb weather allowed us to accomplish much more than we could in the Los Angeles area with its fog and smog. I flew from dawn to two

PM, as many as five flights a day, then retired to the swimming pool or the golf course. In eleven working days I made thirty test flights in the winter in California. Now that's living!

Douglas actually considered installing a test base at Palm Springs, but the city manager would have none of it. Industry was not welcome in this resort town.

The flight envelope for the Skyknight was comparatively small for a jet aircraft. VL, limit dive speed, was 560 mph, which could be achieved in a shallow fifteen degree dive. Service ceiling was 42,000 feet and the design maximum Mach Number was .84, which was attainable in a shallow dive at 30,000 feet. So, demonstrating this aircraft structurally, compared to the problems I had on the AD, was a piece of cake.

One structural demonstration goal was to perform a rolling pull-out at VL, using full aileron deflection. This requires a very skillful maneuver in a propeller driven airplane in a 70 degree dive at limit speed with high roll rates because full aileron throw must be held while the load factor is applied. It is very easy to overshoot the limit load factor while diving, rolling and pulling out almost simultaneously

However, in the Skyknight, VL was obtained easily, and in addition, because of wing twist caused by full aileron deflection, the roll rate was only about 10 degrees per second at 560 mph. It was, therefore, easy to keep all the variables under control. For a fighter, it was mandatory that wing spoilers be installed to correct the deficiency of poor roll rate at high speed.

The demonstration of the maximum safe Mach Number of .845 at 30,000 feet was achieved with the straight wing airplane in a 20 degree dive. I had no control problems but did experience heavy buffeting at the limit Mach. The maximum safe Mach number was placarded to .84 for the service pilots, however, due to this buffet. The F3D's straight and relatively thick wing (for a fighter) and "fat" fuselage were contributing factors to this low rating.

The spins were also a piece of cake, especially the inverted ones because it was impossible to stall the airplane in the inverted position. There was adequate down elevator to meet all other stability and control specifications, so it didn't make any sense to add additional control deflection just to be able to stall the airplane inverted and perform a spin. Consequently, the F3D just swished around when full rudder was applied at the minimum speed attainable. Complete recovery was easily accomplished by merely releasing the displaced controls to allow them to return to the neutral position.

Testing the F3D for hard landings was a dilemma for me. As an Air Force trained pilot I always tried to "grease" the aircraft onto the runway, making the smoothest possible landing. I wanted to hear the gentle squeak of the tires as they met concrete. The Navy's carrier airplanes, however, were built to withstand "controlled crashes" as they slammed onto the flight deck of ships which were not infrequently heaving up and down.

One of the structural demonstration requirements, therefore, was to land the Skyknight at 16 feet per second (fps), the equivalent of 960 feet per minute (fpm), to test the strength of the landing gear and the aircraft itself.

Technique called for lining up on final approach at LAX several miles from the touchdown point. After several build-up flights we realized that ground effect (a cushion-like phenomenon technically described as the effect of the ground in changing the induced airflow over the wings, thus reducing induced drag and increasing lift) was a factor. Even though instrumentation showed that I had properly established a 16 fps sink rate during the approach, ground effect diminished that rate by several fps before impact.

As a result, I had to trim the F3D for a sink rate of 1,200 fpm. Instinctively, however, I was still inclined to pull back on the stick prior to touchdown, which reduced the sink rate even more. So, near touchdown, I forced myself to remove my hand from the stick and hold on to the cockpit structural brace, relying on the aircraft to fly itself onto the runway. With this technique, (which is a hell of way to fly an airplane), I was able to meet the required sink rate. But it took twenty tries. It was unnerving because when the Skyknight hit the concrete it sounded like I had crashed. It was like stalling out of the sky during the final seconds of the landing sequence.

After the last hard landing, I rolled to a stop and began taxiing back to the flight line but couldn't turn the bird. I figured the nose tire had blown, so summoned a tow truck to haul me in.

While waiting for the Douglas crew to arrive I looked around the cockpit and was startled to discover that the nose wheel strut had actually poked up through the cockpit floor immediately adjacent to my right leg!

That evening, as I pulled into my driveway, my neighbor called me over. He had flown in commercially from a trip back east. He said, "I've got to tell you – today I saw a dark blue military aircraft make the worst landings I've ever seen. Terrible!"

I hesitated momentarily then, sheepishly, said, "You were watching me."

He gave me a look of surprise.

"I normally make better landings than what you saw," I said, then explained that all those horrible touchdowns were intentional.

Sometime later, at Edwards Air Force Base, Bill Bridgeman, the test pilot who gained fame flying Ed Heinemann's experimental Skyrocket aircraft, was making hard landing tests in the F4D Skyray. His demonstration point was 21 fps, a 31 percent increase in sink rate over what I had done in the F3D. Bill had asked me what technique I used on the Skyknight. I recounted the key factors, trimming the aircraft, keeping hands off the stick and achieving a sink rate a bit higher than required to counteract ground effect.

Subsequently, I watched Bill perform the tests. On one of them the Skyray impacted the runway, breaking the right landing gear wheel. The jet then skidded off the runway into the dirt. Douglas engineers wondered why the wheel broke at a relatively low sink rate of 12 fps, as indicated by the photoscope. Bill insisted that his vertical velocity indicator was reading much higher than the data the engineers were reading. The engineers reviewed their calibrations and realized they made an error by a factor of two. In other words, he was "sinking" at twice the rate they thought he was.

I was glad to be flying the A4D Skyhawk at this time because at 24 fps, which is equivalent to 1,440 fpm, it was unsettling just to watch the sink rate tests. They really were controlled crashes.

The Navy invited me aboard a carrier to observe F3D-1 carrier qualifications. This was a first for me and I came away thoroughly impressed by the experience. The visit helped me appreciate even more why the Navy had to have aircraft which could land at high sink rates and withstand the associated wear and tear. I enjoyed watching the landings, except for one, made by a pilot in an F2H Banshee. I learned what happens when a carrier pilot "lands short."

In the Air Force, should a pilot fly too low on his approach, he might clip off tree tops or knock down a fence. Aboard the carrier, landing short of the designated touchdown point can be disastrous.

The Banshee was approaching the flattop, too low and slow. The landing signal officer, positioned on a platform to the left of the deck from the pilot's vantage point, frantically signaled to the pilot. Jet engines in those days didn't *spool up* or accelerate quickly, as they do now, plus the pilot was already behind the power curve (with maximum power at high angle of attack he was barely able to maintain flight) and thus helpless to correct his situation.

The Banshee slammed into the fantail. Impact point on the aircraft was right behind the cockpit. The jet exploded, and the front part of the fuselage tumbled down the deck in a ball of fire – with the pilot aboard! It was a heart-stopping, gruesome sight. I didn't think the pilot could possibly survive but incredibly, he did, although badly burned.

The bonus money I received for doing the structural and spin tests on the Skyknight was the easiest I ever earned. The amount was almost twice as much as that for the AD-1, and the F3D demonstration tests were considerably less hazardous to fly. Considering my other experiences, the equation of monetary benefits versus risk was evening out.

The only unusual problems on the F3D-1 were several engine failures, flame-outs from gun gases, loss of the escape door at Pax, hydraulic failures and a failure of the nose wheel landing strut. However, these kinds of deficiencies are to be expected in the flight test business.

In June 1951 I made the first flight in the F3D-2. The -2 was an improved version of the aircraft with wing spoilers and 400 pounds more thrust per engine. The spoilers were added to improve the roll rate at high indicated airspeed. This model was supposed to have the Westinghouse J-46 engine with considerably more thrust, but the engine builders were encountering difficulties and the engine never was installed.

Only twenty-eight F3D-1s were manufactured because of the deficiency in roll rate at high speed. The -2 went into combat in Korea in the autumn of 1952. A key milestone for the Skyknight occurred when it became the first jet night fighter in the Korean War to shoot down an enemy jet airplane at night. It is also one of the few aircraft to see service in both the Korean and Vietnam conflicts.

Shortly after I made the first flight in the F3D-2 things were looking up for me at Douglas. I didn't realize it then, but I was about to be assigned to test a new jet, the bat-wing XF4D Skyray, another Heinemann masterpiece.

8

THE BAT WING FIGHTER

To the victor go the spoils! At the conclusion of World War II in 1945, the Allies raced against time to gather German data, technology and scientists before the Russians made their move. Douglas reaped the fruits of this event when aerodynamicists Gene Root and A.M.O. Smith traveled to Europe as part of a Naval Technical Mission to take a look at German technology. In the process they found a study of tail-less aircraft designs by Dr. Alexander Lippisch. Root and Smith brought back data which complemented tail-less aircraft information the company had been working on since the late 1930s when Jack Northrop, a great proponent of the Flying Wing, was with Douglas.

The data was applied to a wind tunnel program and Ed Heinemann's trusted configuration engineer, Robert G. Smith, made the preliminary design layout.

It was a beautiful machine. The single-place, delta-wing interceptor, looked fast just sitting on the ground.

The XF4D was supposed to be powered by one XJ-40-WE-8 jet engine equipped for after-burning which gave it 11,600 pounds of thrust. The J-40 wasn't immediately available, however, so the initial tests were made with the installation of a 5,000 pound thrust Allison J-35 engine.

Primary pitch and roll control in the Skyray was achieved by use of elevons. An elevon is a control surface which functions both as an elevator and as an aileron. When moving in the same direction, they provide pitch, and when moved differentially, they provide roll.

Longitudinal and lateral trim was obtained from electric trimmers located inboard of the elevons.

The elevons were actuated by a single irreversible hydraulic power control system with artificial *feel* for the pilot, provided by electrical magnetic clutches. A manual flight control system for the elevons was available in the event of hydraulic power failure. Rudder control was achieved manually through the foot pedals, and the prototype had a yaw damper which also actuated the rudder through a servo-system.

The fighter had a unique, four-wheel landing gear which utilized a small, retractable tail wheel to absorb the tail loads during high angle of attack landings and takeoffs.

The wing span was 33.5 feet, the aspect ratio 2.0 (the ratio of length to width), and leading edge sweep-back was 52.5 degrees. The aircraft had aerodynamic, free floating, leading edge slats and horn-balanced, outboard elevons.

Larry Peyton made the first flight in the Skyray on 25 January 1951. At that time I was occupied with finishing the preliminary structural build-up tests on the F3D-1 Skyknight. I spent all of February and March at Pax conducting the formal structural and aerodynamic demonstration and spin tests. After returning to California, I was assigned to test the electronic fuel control on the new J-34-WE38 engine planned for the F3D-2. We also performed the G-3 autopilot and hydraulic pump tests on the bird.

Larry flew the Skyray prototype only once. He was an extremely experienced aviator, especially in large, four-engine transports, but I believe the unusual characteristics of the aircraft's delta-shaped wing and absence of a horizontal tail and only a single-engine were not to his liking. He declined to fly the Skyray again. Moreover, possibly he was bothered by the fact the first flight was intentionally made on manual flight systems resulting in poor control of the airplane.

Russ Thaw was assigned to the fighter, and since the airplane lacked a redundant, hydraulically powered flight control system, one of the early challenges on the project was to determine if the Skyray could be controlled while on the emergency manual flight control system. The control stick could be extended about a foot to enhance mechanical advantage for the pilot, enabling him to move the stick against the air loads on the control surface.

Meanwhile, I had become disenchanted with the F3D-2 electronic tests on the engine fuel control and the autopilot. There were simply too many *gremlins* involved in electronics, and they tended to confound me. Besides, I was anxious to strap on the Skyray. It was dramatically new and exciting as hell.

Fortunately, company officials wanted a second pilot's opinion on the controllability of the Skyray on manual flight control. My opportunity to pilot the fighter had arrived.

Since the airplane was designed to achieve 1.5 Mach Number in a dive, I realized the need for some experience in high Mach airplanes. All that the Air Force had at that time, other than the pure research airplanes, was the F-86, so I requested a checkout in the bird.

On my second flight in the Sabre I evaluated the transonic Mach characteristics. Using military thrust and a 70 degree dive, the plane hit .96 Mach indicated. It exhibited a severe roll-off on the left wing which was uncontrollable. There was no Mach jump on the instrument, but the guys on the ground said that they heard the characteristic sonic boom.

My checkout flight in the Skyray was impressive, especially considering the performance available with the under powered, 5,000-pound thrust J-35 engine. Flight in the low speed range was also memorable. Glen Edwards had once described operating the Northrop flying wing as, "something different." The XF4D was certainly that.

The airplane had excellent visibility over the nose in the landing attitude, so it was very easy to get too slow during approach for landing, and if the pilot wasn't careful the Skyray would descend like a rock. This is an example of what happens if the pilot is on the backside of the power required curve.

The third time out I flew on manual flight control and quickly learned why Larry wanted no part of the Skyray. The stick forces were exorbitant for the small control surface deflection achieved. The plane was tough to handle unless below 200 knots and in smooth air – not a good sign for a fighter which may have to make an approach onto the pitching deck of an aircraft carrier at night.

The Skyray was sent back to the factory for a couple of months for installation of an emergency electrically-driven hydraulic pump and yaw damper. The other prototype was also down, having the J-40 non-after-burning engine installed.

So, during the next three months I flew just about every aircraft Douglas had, performing miscellaneous short term tests. In addition to the AD-4, F3D-2, AD-5 and DC-6, which I had flown before, there were the AD-5W, the Super DC-3, the C-74, the big Air Force cargo plane, the C-124 (a bigger cargo plane which I didn't like at all), the Bonanza, the Navion, and the Navy R4D-8. I also flew short hops to the desert transporting engineers or parts.

One day I was assigned to go as copilot in the R4D-8 for a high-speed, rolling-pullout test because the project pilot had never performed this maneuver. The plane, the Navy's version of the Super DC-3, had bigger engines than the regular DC-3, was 50 mph faster, had a bigger tail, retractable tail wheel, and carried 30 passengers. In a fighter with high roll rate, high speed, high load factor and high dive angle, this maneuver requires practice because it is difficult to achieve all the parameters at the same time. In the lumbering, medium size transport, it was a piece of cake because the maneuver consisted of only a 30-degree dive, 30-degree per second roll rate and a 2.0 G pullout.

In January 1952 the XF4D returned to flight status. I flew a few more manual control flight tests. In fact, at one time I had more flight hours on manual than on powered-flight control. Under ideal conditions I could actually land the Skyray on manual without touching the stick by using the rudder for roll and the trimmers for pitch control. In any case, Douglas decided to design a redundant hydraulic control system for production models of the F4D.

At approach speed, there simply was too much adverse yaw when rolling – it actually reversed the roll. Adverse yaw means that when rolling in one direction, the airplane yaws in the opposite direction. If directional stability is weak, and if the airplane's dihedral effect is high – which means it can be rolled with yaw – the resultant effect is an undamped, rolling/yawing oscillation called a "Dutch Roll."

For example. in the power approach (PA) configuration at 113 knots with the yaw damper off and the pilot's feet off the rudder pedals, a roll rate reversal can occur. This would cause the Skyray to roll in the opposite direction as adverse yaw increases. The free manual rudder also will float with the relative airstream, which also reduces the roll rate.

The adverse yaw could be reduced somewhat with the yaw damper, but since it was a manual rudder, the feedback into the rudder pedals was considered unsatisfactory during the Navy Preliminary Evaluation. I determined that the adverse yaw with roll could be eliminated if the pilot provided a large rudder input. Unfortunately, I could not convince the NPE pilots that they should coordinate a turn with the rudder as they had been taught in basic flight school.

Since the flight controls were moved by hydraulic power, an artificial force-feel system was mandatory for the pilot and was provided by means of electric magnetic clutches. The force gradient was not linear, and the clutches caused a grabbing effect resulting in erratic flight.

One day I was trying to determine elevon position from trim speed data in order to determine the degree of static longitudinal stability. The clutches were grabbing such that I couldn't hold a constant airspeed. Since the air was smooth, I elected to bypass the force feel system by turning the switch off, so the flight wouldn't be a complete waste. This was fine until I inadvertently flew into someone's prop or jet wash. The turbulence jostled my arm so that it moved the now "zero force" control stick, resulting in an inadvertent and uncomfortable imposition of 5 Gs on the Skyray. I quickly activated the erratic force-feel system and terminated the flight. All fighter pilots like low control forces so that they can maneuver the airplane easily, but not ZERO force!

Since we had to use the J-35 engine in the Skyray on the exploratory flight tests in the transonic realm, I had to push over into shallow dives around 35,000 feet. There was moderately severe tuck-under in the transonic regime beginning at Mach 0.91. A large amount of pitch trimmer deflection was needed because of the reduced control effectiveness of the elevons, which produced high trim drag. On top of that, transonic shock wave also caused tail buffet and rudder buzz.

We tried a number of tail cone configurations, fourteen as a matter of fact, in an attempt to "clean up" the aircraft. In the first revision, with the J-35 installed, we placed a blunt trailing edge fairing beneath the rudder while removing the fairing behind the tail wheel. In the second we replaced the tail wheel fairing and extended the fairing behind the rudder. The final refinement extended the top fairing aft of the tailpipe. This configuration allowed us to continue the transonic development program to Mach .94.

In February, 1952, the airplane with the J-40 engine, but without afterburner, was ready for flight, thirteen months late. With 7,000 pounds of thrust the Skyray could now climb to altitude much quicker than before for the high Mach investigation. Also, dive angles did not have to be as steep to attain transonic speed. However, we ran into the same problems with buffet and rudder buzz and had to start all over again, designing new tail cones for this engine.

We had been holding the Navy off from evaluating the airplane because we needed to ensure its supersonic capabilities. That meant having the J-40 *with the afterburner.* After all, this was the engine the Navy contracted for, and without the afterburner the Skyray would lack the necessary performance.

Since it was a year-and-a-half from the first flight, the Navy insisted on evaluating the plane because it had placed a production order for 230 F4Ds a few months before. They were well aware of the problems we were confronting and wanted to determine if the problem was, in fact, viable.

The airplane was placarded to .95 Mach with the rudder locked mechanically above .92 Mach and 637 mph for the NPE team which consisted of Marine Major Marion Carl, Commander Bob Elder and Lieutenant Commander Bob Clark – all terrific aviators. They flew the bird and were impressed with its maneuvering capabilities at high altitude. The buffet boundary during turns at 40,000 feet was 3.4 Gs at Mach .9; 3.2 Gs at Mach .8; and 3.0 Gs at Mach .7. All of the Air Force chase airplanes immediately fell out of the sky during these maneuvers.

I can distinctly remember Carl's comment at the completion of the evaluation. He said, "If we had this airplane now in Korea, I could just pop off the MiGs – one, two, three."

We had problems with the electronic fuel control on the J-40 engine. Sometimes it would go to idle when the throttle was pushed forward to full military thrust, and sometimes it would go to max thrust when the throttle was retarded to idle. Until we fixed this it was necessary to keep one finger on the manual fuel control switch for immediate reversion during take-off and landing.

Corky Meyer, chief test pilot for Grumman, was flying his company's XF10F with the same engine at the time. We occasionally met to compare notes and got on the subject of manual fuel control. Corky said, tongue in cheek, he wanted a large gate valve installed in the middle of the cockpit so that when he needed more fuel all he had to do was reach out and turn the valve.

After the NPE our first priority remained to get the airplane supersonic. Ironically, when we reached that milestone – a first for a delta-wing aircraft – I was unaware of it because the Mach meter indicated only .97. While climbing for another dive to attain an increase in speed one of the engineers radioed, "Were you heading toward the base when you made that dive?"

"Affirmative," I replied.

"We heard the boom," he said. I had gone supersonic. I was elated, of course, as this was a moment of historic significance in the life of the Skyray.

I increased the dive angle by five degrees for the next try. The characteristic jump in Mach Number to 1.02 at about 30,000 feet was deeply satisfying, even to the most pessimistic of observers. We had achieved this landmark after a year-and-a-half of test flights. Plus, it occurred less than one month after the Navy's first NPE.

The Skyray was designed to fly supersonic at sea level, so even with the non-after-burning J-40 engine, tail buffet and rudder buzz emerged again as a problem at high dynamic pressure (high indicated airspeed), a dilemma that was to endure for a long time.

Again, we had to experiment with tail cone configurations. It took months to resolve this problem and approximately 150 dives.

Qualitatively evaluating eleven different tail cones with the J-40 engine was a mind-boggling exercise, as the engineers continually asked me to compare one configuration with several others. It was finally decided to install telemetry to assist me during this exploratory period and to allow realtime evaluation by the engineers, which also enhanced safety. The telemetry permitted the engineers to determine immediately if the aircraft was approaching its structural limits.

On the first telemetry flight my objective was to get the sonic boom at 10,000 feet. Chuck Yeager was the assigned chase pilot. I got in position at altitude and began the dive. I was bound and determined to continue downward until the test engineer monitoring the telemetry told me to pull out. The Skyray began to buffet severely and rudder buzz was at high amplitude when I chickened out and pulled up – at a point which precisely coincided with the engineer's command to "Pull up, now!"

Yeager, who was glued to my wing, was unaware that the flight was being monitored by telemetry and was startled by the command from the ground. A moment later he transmitted to me, "I saw the high amplitude rudder buzz, Bob, but I sure didn't think it was bad enough for the guys on the ground to see it with the naked eye, from 10,000 feet away!"

"Sorry, Chuck," I apologized, laughing to myself, "I forgot to tell you, this is our first flight with telemetry. They saw the buzz on the gauges." I could almost feel Chuck's astonishment in the other cockpit.

Probably because of the other difficulties we had with the Skyray's unconventional design, I approached the spin tests with unusual caution. No one had ever spun a delta-wing aircraft before, so we were in virgin territory. At the same time, I had never feared spinning airplanes because if trouble occurred, there were always two means of escape – the spin chute, and if that didn't work, bail-out or ejection.

Truth is, I enjoyed spins. I figured it was me against the airplane, much like a cowboy riding a bucking bronco, and was determined to best the beast.

The plan was to perform one five-turn spin at a forward cg with the J-35 engine to determine early in the program whether any major aerodynamic redesign was necessary. Concerns were alleviated somewhat when, on a March 1952 flight, I spun the XF4D for the first time and, using the conventional technique of opposite rudder and neutral stick, made an uneventful recovery. The work-up phase consisted of a half turn at a time, up to two turns, and then a full turn increase each time until the required five turns were accomplished.

Al Carder, who was the Test Project Coordinator at the time and who was cautious by nature, was more concerned about the outcome of the spin tests than I was. He observed the spins from the ramp outside the flight office. After a few work-up spins I radioed that the yaw damper was producing heavy rudder pedal forces by applying opposite rudder to correct for the high yaw angles that resulted with full pedal deflection.

Al suggested a return to base, but I just turned the yaw damper off and continued with the spins. After several more work-up spins, he radioed that I ought to come on home because I was probably getting tired. Actually, he was getting nervous and just wanted the Skyray back on the ground in one piece. He tried a third time, explaining that I must be low on fuel which was not the case. I was flying at high altitude where consumption is less, plus the spins were done at idle throttle. He said my gauges must be inaccurate. Nevertheless, I stayed aloft and finished the required tests.

Several months later the J-40 was installed and we resumed the spin program with a more aft center of gravity. This led to increased oscillations in pitch, roll and yaw. Also, reversals in spin direction occurred even while holding in full pro-spin controls. Additionally, the number of turns required for recovery increased.

After the first few work-up spins in the renewed program, I attempted to make two turns to the left in the spin. The Skyray had its own agenda, spun one and a half turns then reversed direction, even as I held full pro-spin controls (full left rudder and full aft stick). The jet began a slow flat spin to the right. I tried to recover by holding in left rudder and neutralizing the stick. However, the XF4D rolled abruptly upside down and started spinning inverted. Such spins, as every aviator knows, are hazardous to one's health. A cardinal rule, true as much today as then, is, simply put: "Avoid circumstances which might lead to an inverted spin." Indeed, I had never even been in one before in any airplane. I had tried, without success, to do so in the F3D, but that was for test purposes.

In the inverted mode I experienced severe oscillations in pitch as much as 120 degrees in a half turn and fell through the sky upside down. At this extreme attitude in pitch I had the impression I was actually in a 60 degree nose-down, upright spin. For a moment I was totally perplexed. Was I or wasn't I inverted? I wasn't even sure which direction the aircraft was spinning until I felt the high rudder pedal forces.

Since the rudder was manual (not power boosted) I was applying maximum pilot effort on the rudder pedal just to return the pedal to the neutral position.

Anyway, things got worse, although I didn't realize it at the time. The ejection seat broke loose from its mounting due to the high negative load factor and became pressed against the canopy. I wasn't aware of it because it was of trivial concern compared to the main problem of recovering the airplane.

Down we came. Pre-planned spin chute deployment altitude was 10,000 feet. As the altimeter needle swung through that height it was evident that help was needed. I pulled the release handle and the chute shot out from the tail and ballooned with a reassuring tug. Within a few seconds the chute was able to stabilize the machine although I was now diving vertically and running out of altitude but fortunately, at a slow speed. I released the spin chute and pulled the stick back, leveling off at 4,000 feet (1,800 feet above the ground) – quite a drop since the maneuver started at 36,000 feet.

It felt very good to get back on the ground. As if to add an exclamation point to the flight, however, as I was taxiing back in I discovered I could not open the canopy. I shivered with the realization that had the spin chute not worked, with the ejection seat dislodged from its mounting, there was no way to escape. I could have been entombed in the Skyray. I wiped the cold sweat off of my brow while waiting for the mechanics to remove the canopy from the airplane.

In retrospect, I have often wondered how many turns I did, but the chase pilot did not have a cameraman. I did some calculations, and figuring a loss of about 1,000 feet per turn in a controlled spin, the aircraft must have made about thirty turns during the *inverted* crisis. Fate must have been watching every turn and decided that I had had enough for one day.

Upon reviewing the flight recorder, Steve Tydeman, the flight test engineer, informed me that I pushed 560 pounds on the rudder pedal. This was amazing. I had applied 300 pounds on the pedals during earlier structural sideslips, which was less than maximum human effort, but the most for which the system was designed. Considering the 1.5 safety factor inherent in the design, the system should have failed at 450 pounds.

The adrenaline was really flowing, and apparently I had more strength than thought possible, like the mother lifting an automobile from a trapped child.

We went back to the drawing board (spin tunnel, actually), to figure out a more positive recovery technique. We examined the movies of the XF4D model in the tunnel. I became quite apprehensive when the tests confirmed that the F4D's spin characteristics were dramatically erratic. But we also discovered that recovery characteristics, using aileron as the primary recovery control, would be more positive. The term, aileron, in this case is used to describe the differential deflection of the elevons for lateral control.

I was a bit fearful about resuming the spin program, but a stronger spin chute, designed to withstand greater opening shock loads, was installed in the aircraft, and that put me in a better frame of mind. It was important that the pilot master the airplane instead of the other way around. I requested we make every effort to get in two flights per day so that I could maintain this positive mind set.

With respect to the anxiety I experienced at this point in the program, I should explain my interpretation of fear and fright. To me, they are separate entities. Fear takes time to grow, usually over a period of helpless inactivity. Fear is contagious and can be a preamble to panic. It takes time to recover from fear. Fright, on the other hand, is only the initial impact of fear. It's instantaneous. It is a physical reaction to a trying situation rather than an emotional one. It can strike, explode and be gone quickly. Fright is unpredictable yet when it occurs, clear thinking is possible in response. The actuation of a pilot's muscles and joints can accelerate unbelievably in response to fright which, I think, accounts for the ability of a test pilot to handle emergencies that might otherwise be catastrophic. I may have feared the spin tests but fright was my state of mind in the uncontrolled spins and it disappeared with successful deployment of the chute.

Ailerons were the primary recovery control because their deflection with the spin created a roll rate which allowed positive pitch and produced a yawing moment in the opposite direction to help terminate the spin. The technical term for this is inertia coupling.   I hadn't fully understood inertia coupling, although I was familiar with it at high speeds, when it caused airplanes to go out of control. Yet I could not comprehend how it applied to a *stalled* airplane. I reasoned that the airplane had high adverse yaw with roll at slow speed and the resultant yawing moment was enough to terminate the spin. This was an incorrect analogy, but Mal Abzug, the engineer who did the spin tunnel tests, didn't pursue his explanation as long as I agreed to use the new technique.

To determine spin direction and when to neutralize controls, I used the needle of the turn and bank indicator. It was the primary recovery instrument. We found that the rudder was virtually ineffective in an upright spin because it was blanketed from the airstream by the wing. In an inverted spin, the high yaw and floating rudder required extremely high force just to bring the rudder back to the neutral position.

The reason for retaining full aft stick during the recovery from an upright spin was to keep the aircraft in a positive, stalled attitude to prevent an unplanned inverted spin.

I entered the spins in many different ways. There was the conventional method with power off. In the normal rated thrust entry, I didn't retard the throttle until the completion of a half-turn which invariably produced compressor stalls of the engine. I actually saw flame coming out of the inlet air ducts. Some spins were entered from an inverted attitude, and some by executing snap rolls at 150 knots which occasionally produced a spin. I flew spins holding one-third aileron with and against the rotation while in the spin. Accelerated 2.5 G stall entries were performed where the airplane did not spin until rudder was applied. Finally, I executed spins with external stores on board plus 300 gallon tanks loaded with 200 gallons of fuel to change the inertia of the airplane.

Nevertheless, spin characteristics of the Skyray remained somewhat erratic. Very seldom would the aircraft settle into a nice steady spin. They were highly oscillatory in pitch, yaw and roll, and quite frequently I experienced spin reversal, even when holding full pro-spin controls.

After about 150 spins in the F4D a technique was proven which assured satisfactory recovery. I had to adhere to the following procedures:

(1) Determine the direction of the spin by the needle of the turn and bank indicator

(2) (a) For upright spins, use opposite rudder, full aileron *with* the spin and full back stick.

(b) For inverted spins use opposite rudder as much as possible and full aileron *against* the spin with neutral stick.

(3) When the needle of the turn and bank indicator leaves the peg, neutralize controls *immediately* or a reversal will occur.

The above procedure is complicated for the average service pilot and took a lot of practice even for me. By the time the program was completed, I was quite adept at using the technique and could perform the recovery completely by the use of instruments only. In fact, I could do it better when on the gauges because the turn and bank indicator needle was much more sensitive to yaw than my body. Once the needle left the pegged position, recovery was just a matter of neutralizing the controls.

In the years that followed a few airplanes were lost because of inadvertent spins by Navy pilots. Even one of Douglas' production test pilots had to eject from a Skyray because of an inadvertent spin. Because of these losses I became a movie star of sorts, a prime actor in a training film on how to recover from a spin. With film in hand I visited several Skyray squadrons and briefed the aviators on spin recovery techniques.

At the completion of the formal spin demonstration at Pax, the airplane with the spin chute installed was transferred to the Navy. The Navy seriously considered using it as a training vehicle for the pilots, but that never came to fruition. This was a mistake because every fighter pilot should experience the limits of his airplane before going into combat, and spinning the airplane was, in this sense, a limit that should have been explored by a military pilot.

The second NPE was held in November 1952 and the result was reassuring: the airplane was ready for the fleet and Lieutenant Commander Jim Verdin was selected for the carrier suitability trials held in the Spring of 1953.

After the second Navy evaluation, the Air Force became interested in the Skyray and asked to fly the airplane. Chuck Yeager, Pete Everest and Slade Nash were the three selected. I gave Chuck the flight manuals in preparation for his first flight. I don't know if he read them, but the next day he climbed into the plane for a cockpit checkout. As I stood on the boarding ladder pointing out the switches and gauges I could tell Chuck wasn't listening because he impatiently glanced at his wrist watch every couple of minutes.

After awhile, Yeager said, "Forget this crap, Bob. Just show me where the throttle is."

I shook my head but didn't let his eagerness to get on with it dissuade me from completing the checkout. I purposely pointed out that with its delta wing the Skyray had a very high angle of attack near the stall speed and that the curve at maximum lift coefficient was very flat which made it difficult to ascertain when a stall would occur.

I cautioned Chuck, "If you're going to do any approach to stalls requiring high angle of attack flying, don't do them for long duration while on low fuel. If you do, you'll unport the fuel outlet from the tanks, and the engine will flame out!" I repeated this several times during the briefing.

Chuck and the XF4D launched into the burning blue and sure enough, after evaluating the airplane for awhile, he flew at a high angle of attack with low fuel in the tanks. The engine flamed out, and Yeager had to deadstick the Skyray down to the lake bed at Muroc.

The Air Force was impressed with the Skyray, and would have liked to have it in its inventory, but the delta wing F-102 interceptor was coming along soon. Anyway, Douglas could not meet the deadline set by the Air Force because production demands on earlier commitments to the Navy precluded timely delivery. The production lines at El Segundo were filled to capacity with four types of airplanes – two fighters and two attack.

The A2D Skyshark and the XF4D Skyray had identical, slide-back canopy systems. The engineers wanted to determine why the Skyshark canopy did not open fully in flight when Livingston lost the props and gear box, so the test was assigned to me in the Skyray. While airborne, I actuated the lever and the canopy slid back. But something was wrong. It slid back too far.

"The canopy's gone back farther than normal," I radioed to the engineers.

After a pause during which I pictured the engineers running through the technical manuals, an alarming report came back to me. "Bob, be advised, you may have a hot seat!"

A hot seat meant that the ejection seat could activate at any instant, firing me into that burning blue. This was not good for the nerves. I didn't panic, but I was sure wary. With great care I guided the fighter back onto the runway at Edwards, executing one of the smoothest landings of my career. Happily, the seat didn't fire, but upon examining the canopy, the engineers verified that it might very well have cooked off. This gave the engineers plenty to think about. Doc couldn't get his canopy to open far enough and mine opened too far.

I got the biggest bang out of flying the delta wing jet fighter in formation with the company's Navion, which was a general aviation, single-engine type with a 260 horsepower engine. The purpose was to calibrate the fighter's airspeed system at high angle of attack and slow speed.

The Skyray's approach speed was the Navion's cruise speed. At maximum endurance speed for the Navion (that speed requiring *minimum* power to stay in level flight) at 75 knots, the F4D had to use nearly maximum military power because it was on the wrong side of the power-required curve.

At extremely high alpha (angle of attack) near the stall, the "ship was sinking" even using afterburner if it didn't blow out or experience a compressor stall first, and I couldn't keep up with the low-powered Navion. I've always wished I had a photo of that flight. We looked like the Odd Couple, or Mutt and Jeff.

9

LEGALIZED BUZZING

I helped aviation writer Nicholas M. Williams put together an article on the F4D which focused on the Skyray's record-breaking attempts and successes. Nick was then an Associate Editor of the *Journal of the American Aviation Historical Society*, a wonderful publication and organization. I have revised somewhat the resultant article from the Spring 1976 edition of the *Journal* and offer it here as it chronicles the quest of Douglas and the Navy for World Speed and Time to Climb records.

A flurry of speed records were being set across the country and in Europe. In November, 1952 an F-86D piloted by Captain J. Slade Nash set a new three kilometer record by averaging 698.505 mph on a course set up by North American Aviation Co. over the shores of the Salton Sea in Southern California. Jacqueline Cochran made the headlines in May of 1953 by flying a Canadian-built F-86 to a new 100 km closed course speed record of 652.337 mph over a route she had personally set up at Edwards. Like the Olympics, these records were measured right down to the thousandths.

Two months later the three kilometer record was broken by the Air Force as Lieutenant Colonel William F. Barnes flew his F-86D over the Salton Sea course, averaging 715.7 mph. To further re-emphasize their air superiority, the Air Force broke the 100 km record again on September 2nd when Brigadier General J. Stanley Holtoner piloted his F-86D over the closed course at Vandalia, Ohio at 689.8 mph. The American record-setting was cut short, however, as England entered the headlines a few weeks later. On September 7th, Squadron Leader Neville F. Duke set a new 3 km record in England by piloting a Hawker Hunter with a 729 mph average. On September 19th, he surpassed the 100 km closed course record by averaging 709 mph average in the same aircraft.

Thus, in little less than a year, six new records had been set at the three kilometer and 100 kilometer distances alone. As reports of other aircraft and countries' preparations for record attempts became known, the aviation world became charged with the excitement of competition. The stage was set for the Navy and Douglas to step in with the Skyray.

It's uncertain as to how long they had been thinking of the challenge. As one of his assignments, Robert B. Smith, a Douglas engineer, had the job of determining what world records any El Segundo-designed aircraft could set. Whenever someone wished to try for a speed record and have the results officially recognized, they had to notify the world governing body for all air speed records, the Paris-based Federation Aeronautique Internationale (F.A.I.), pay a sanction fee, and submit the aircraft to an official inspection team to insure that it conformed to the rules that separated the various classes of aircraft. The course also had to be certified as being laid out accurately. In the United States the F.A.I.'s representative, the National Aeronautics Asso ciation (NAA) and its officials, timed and recorded the speed attempts made in this country. If successful, the speeds or times were forwarded to the F.A.I. for official registration.

In late summer, 1953, Ed Heinemann decided to try for the three kilometer record. This relatively short (1.86 mile) straight-away course had long been recognized as the classic event by which aircraft were compared. The best average speed from four passes over the course was considered the world's absolute speed record, as opposed to other records for class of aircraft used or distance around a circular course.

Preparations began in mid-August at the Douglas testing facilities at Edwards. The three kilometer course at Edwards was Air Force property so Douglas requested, and received, permission for its use. On September 14th Douglas submitted its formal application for the speed attempt to the NAA requesting that official observers, timers and their equipment be furnished at Edwards.

Shortly thereafter, North American Aviation also submitted an application for the three kilometer record. Upon learning of the Douglas intent, North American officials naturally felt that their new F-100 should have been given the first chance at the record. The Skyray, they reasoned, had not even had the after-burning J-40 engine installed and had yet to exceed 650 mph. The YF-100, on the other hand, had been equipped with the after-burning J-57 for some time, regularly flying in the 750 mph range. However, NAA insisted that Douglas and the Skyray had the right to make the first attempt by virtue of the earlier application date and that they would retain this priority until October 15, 1953.

Thirty-five year old Jim Verdin, who had flown carrier trials in the Skyray, was a World War II and Korean combat pilot with over 100 missions in his log book, was selected to make the try. A trim, handsome man, Verdin looked the part of a test pilot, and the Navy took full advantage of this in publicity photographs and films of the event.

But the more immediate chore of getting the F4D ready for the speed runs fell to Douglas. By mid-September, the after-burning J-40-WE-8 was finally installed in the XF4D, and the record attempt was scheduled for Saturday, September 26th. Flight test personnel are usually considered pessimistic, but for this project we were extremely optimistic with the Skyray. We had eleven working days to install the engine, increase speed by 100 mph, evaluate stability and control on the deck, prepare a flight plan, and become familiar with the course.

I made the first unrestricted afterburner flight on the 20th and to everyone's surprise, the engine worked flawlessly. After only three test hops with the after-burning engine, I flew the Skyray over the three kilometer course at 100 feet of altitude. Bringing the XF4D down on the deck at military power, I lined up with a long strip of black asphalt recently applied to the course on the dry lake bed to aid visibility.

Approaching the "entrance," I advanced the throttle beyond the détente in the throttle quadrant, igniting the afterburner. I felt a powerful push to my backside as the Skyray quickly accelerated to over 700 mph. The test airplanes had sensitive airspeed indicators which could be read to plus or minus one mph. I had never flown at such a high IAS before and when that big "7" showed up on the dial, I was exhilarated. The desert floor, a mere 100 feet below, became a blur and the airplane started buffeting from the rough air as it approached the speed of sound.

For an instant I was terrified. "What the hell am I doing here?" I said to myself.

The Skyray suddenly yawed uncontrollably and skidded violently off the course. I cut the burner and pulled up, climbing for altitude, testing the controls as I did so. I brought the bird back to a landing, shut down and climbed out. The engineers flocked around the Skyray and right away we saw what caused the yaw. A metal shroud covering the tail wheel had peeled back into the air stream during the high speed run. That was easily repaired.

Brigadier General Holtoner, an early speed record holder who was Commanding General of Edwards AFB, appeared one day when we were preparing for the three kilometer record attempt. He singled me out and asked me a number of questions about the XF4D. He was especially curious about the Skyray's controllability, explaining that he didn't want a Navy aircraft crashing on his base. The Air Force had tested the experimental delta-wing Convair XF-92 with Chuck Yeager, General Boyd, Colonel Pete Everest and Kit Murray being the only military pilots allowed to fly it because of its difficult and unusual handling qualities. I convinced the general that the Skyray was as sound as a dollar, so he elected not to put any restrictions on us. I recall thinking that was the first and only time a general ever *came to see me*. Usually, it was the other way around.

I flew five more high speed flights in the next couple of days, determining the proper handling technique and the number of seconds of allowable afterburner time, which was critical. It was necessary during these runs to fly the plane with a fixed longitudinal trim setting. This was due to rapid acceleration and deceleration with the afterburner on or off. The pilot simply did not have time to worry about trim at such fast airspeeds. This resulted in a tuck under, or nose down pitch, while flying at transonic speed in afterburner, and a nose up pitch condition while using military power. The odd result was that I had to exert a *pull* force on the stick while in *level* flight and a *push* force during the steeply banked *turns*.

Controlling the airplane in the turnaround was also tricky. Stringent F.A.I. rules prevented the aircraft from exceeding 500 meters (1,640 feet) in the turns. In order to conserve fuel, I had to cut the afterburner the instant I passed out of the course, and bank around in a wide, low turn at 650 mph, which required a five-mile diameter to return to the course. This rule was originally intended to stop aircraft from diving into the course to gain speed.

To get as much fuel as possible into the Skyray's tanks, the Douglas crew piped the JP-4 through coils immersed in alcohol packed with dry ice. This reduced the fuel temperature to about 35 degrees Fahrenheit, which also reduced its volume.

While I was testing the Skyray with its new engine, Jim Verdin flew an F9F Cougar from the Naval Air Auxiliary Station, El Centro, California. He piloted it over the course several times to familiarize himself with landmarks.

After only one hour and 55 minutes flight time in the afterburner-equipped Skyray, we turned the airplane over to Jim. It was Friday, September 25th. Up to this date, the best speed I had recorded over the course was a

737 mph average which established a new unofficial, world speed record. Unknown to us at the time, however, on the same day, September 25th, in 103 degree heat in the Libyan Desert, England's Mike Lithgow had flown the same speed over a three kilometer course. Piloting a Vickers Supermarine Swift with a cockpit packed with dry ice, Lithgow had broken Neville Duke's record with a 737.3 mph average.

Back in the Mojave Desert, Jim Verdin used the day to make several high speed familiarization flights in the Skyray. He felt ready for the attempt by Friday afternoon so the go-ahead was given for an official try next day, the original target date. A 35 mph wind dashed the effort, however, kicking up clouds of sand so thick that visibility was questionable and turbulence dangerous. To assess the situation, Verdin and I flew over the course in a company Navion and decided to cancel.

We called a conference that afternoon and decided to take advantage of predicted higher temperatures in the Salton Sea area, 140 miles south of Edwards. North American graciously gave Douglas permission to use its privately owned course, along with timing equipment and technicians.

Verdin flew to El Centro in his Cougar while I ferried the XF4D to the base. I was to fly the Skyray through the course at maximum speed before landing. Since the Salton Sea course was actually below sea level, some 2,600 feet lower than the one at Edwards, there would be an expected rise in the indicated airspeed of about 20 mph. It would be interesting, I thought, to find out the effects, if any, this would have on the handling of the airplane.

I was accelerating across the east side of the sea when a pronounced yaw developed at about five mph below max speed. While trying to determine the cause and whether or not the yaw could be trimmed out, the XF4D skidded all the way across the sea to the west side!

Upon landing we discovered that a piece of skin in the wing root had raised up. We "nailed" the piece back down which reduced the yaw somewhat, but it was never completely eliminated, and we never did find out what else was causing it. Worse, I couldn't trim it out. Nevertheless, Verdin decided to take the aircraft "as is" for the record attempt.

By now we had learned about Lithgow's achievement in the Libyan desert and were rather disheartened. My best unofficial run at Edwards was no faster than Lithgow's, but we decided to try anyway since we believed the Swift's record might still be unofficial, and we could fly faster at the new, low altitude course with its characteristic higher temperatures.

Due to mechanical problems, it was another two days before Jim got airborne and completed four officially timed passes, but not without further mishap. Flying the course late that afternoon, when the temperature was below 90 degrees, the first three passes were satisfactory enough: 748.4 and 746.9 mph on the downwind passes and 740.8 mph on the first upwind run.

On the final upwind pass, at the end of the course, however, Verdin pulled up unexpectedly. The engine had fluctuated due to fuel starvation to the afterburner.

"The gauges did a little dance," Jim told reporters, "and I thought I'd better head for someplace to land. But it settled down and flew just great on the basic (sans afterburner) engine."

The slow last pass of 734.6 mph brought Verdin's average down to 742.7. He needed 744.6 to beat the British mark by the required one percent.

However, as it was still not known that the Swift's record of 737 mph was officially recognized and therefore the speed to beat, there was some agonizing decision-making by Navy and Douglas officials on whether or not to submit the 742.7 mph run as an official attempt.

There were several factors to be considered. The Navy and Douglas were both eager to submit because it would be the first time in US naval aviation history that a carrier aircraft had held a world speed record. However, the pro was overbalanced by some cons. It was all too apparent that North American was waiting with its F-100, and would probably beat the XF4D mark on the first try. The Supermarine Swift was also preparing for another try at the record, and Hawker was reportedly taking its Hunter down to the Libyan Desert to make an official attempt at the three kilometer record. Despite these considerations, we *knew* the Skyray could do better than the 742 mph average and decided not to submit the speed as an official attempt.

Adding to the tension surrounding these matters, transatlantic telephone calls were exchanged between London and El Centro and also from Paris, headquarters of the F.A.I., to Thermal, California, where the NAA timers had set up their headquarters. Therefore, we knew that the British were closely following our progress. Exacerbating the strain on the other side of the Atlantic, we refrained from providing information as to what speeds we were obtaining or when we would make an official try. For their part, the British were not about to give their American competitors any indication of their progress either.

After the record attempt on Tuesday I flew the XF4D back to El Segundo for minor repairs to the afterburner and to patch some tears in the wing skin and tail cone. The next try was set for Friday, when higher temperatures were predicted for the Salton Sea area. We were after true airspeed and didn't care about indicated airspeed (IAS), only the time it took to go from A to B. The hotter it was the higher the true airspeed we could achieve. The mechanics took advantage of the delay by completely reworking the aircraft. Every hole in the Skyray was sealed over, the wing slats sealed, the arresting hook and tail wheel removed, and every protuberance smoothed out or removed. The plane was waxed to the point that it really looked like a "racer."

When rework on the Skyray had been completed at El Segundo, the pressure was on to fly the bird back to El Centro as soon as possible for the expected high temperatures on Friday. Once again, though, weather conspired to delay the attempt. A thick fog had settled over the Los Angeles Airport, precluding any takeoff by the XF4D. It was a Douglas rule that no test plane would be flown in instrument weather.

The tight schedule of the record try, however, led me to convince my boss that I could hold the airplane on the deck after lift off, accelerate to high speed and zoom up through the fog in a matter of seconds. The overcast was about 200 feet, the tops 1,000 feet. He agreed to let me go, but there were many a back turned and fingers crossed when I took the airport runway, added power, and took off. I got airborne, held the Skyray on the deck briefly, accelerated rapidly to 300 plus knots, then hauled back on the stick. Up we went through the fog bank and no more than a couple of seconds later, I burst into the clear and aimed toward El Centro.

On the way, I made another maximum speed run over the Salton Sea course and achieved an encouraging higher indicated airspeed.

The expected high temperatures on Friday never materialized. Although the thermometer climbed into the low 90s, it was still too "cool" for an all-out attempt at the record. A temperature of around 98 degrees F would put the speed of sound at approximately 792 mph. The XF4D was going to need all the help it could get to set a record because we had just learned that the Swift's record was official, and had to be bettered by the required one percent. This meant that Jim would have to average 745 mph and temperatures around the 100 degree mark would be vital for success. So we rescheduled the flight for the next day, Saturday, October 3rd, and began sweating out a warm day.

Next day we plotted the winds and air temperature at the Salton Sea every half hour. Not surprisingly, this clearly showed an increase in air temperature with the decrease in wind velocity. Encouraged, Verdin manned his F9F and made a test run over the course. He reported that the turbulence was not excessive. The world speed record attempt was on.

As the temperature gradually rose toward the 100 degree mark, the crew hurriedly prepared the Skyray for flight. I spent the last hour with Verdin in "solitary" – an empty room containing a couple of bunks. We talked about things totally unrelated to flying.

At 3:00 p.m., as the temperature peaked at 98.5 degrees, Jim strapped himself into the fighter, which had been loaded with 4,550 pounds of pre-cooled fuel (400 pounds more than normal). It was 3:22 p.m. when he headed north toward the course. After a few minutes, he brought the XF4D up to full military power when he could see identifying smoke from the burning tires in the distance. Still several miles from the entrance to the course, he lit the afterburner. The plane accelerated to its maximum speed just as he entered the traps.

By unofficial watches, Verdin's first pass against the wind was a relatively slow 745 mph, just barely fast enough to capture the world record, but the downwind runs would more than make up for this.

Each time the XF4D whipped through the course and started its turn-around Verdin radioed his remaining fuel to the engineers. There was real concern he might not have enough fuel left to make it back to El Centro.

Verdin's next three runs went as smoothly as the first. The Skyray performed beautifully but only the official's photos, timing devices and measurements would tell if a new speed record had been set.

After exchanging congratulations, Jim, myself and some of the Douglas management flew from El Centro aboard a company DC-3 to the Thermal Airport, 30 miles north of the speed course. Here, NAA officials were beginning the tedious process of developing the films taken of the flight. They had to measure the pictures and compute the Skyray's speed using slide rules, magnifying glasses, and a comptometer. It was incongruous that these highly technical procedures were conducted in a dingy back room of the airport's office building. As darkness approached, a naked, 50-watt bulb burned over the small wooden table where the timers had their equipment spread out. Broken glass lay by the windows and paint was peeling from the walls.

Observing this scene of tired and unkempt men huddled around the dimly lit room, I said to myself, "We appear more like bandits dividing our loot than officials from the National Aeronautic Association figuring out a new world speed record."

The computational process took nearly six hours, but the wait was well worth it. The photos showed that the Skyray had indeed broken the record. With passes of 745.075, 761.414, 746.053, and 759.499 mph, Verdin had averaged a remarkable 753.4 mph to give the United States the absolute world speed record over the three kilometer distance.

To me it was noteworthy that the upwind passes only had a delta difference of .98 mph and the downwind passes a difference of 1.91 mph. This was further evidence of the so called sonic "brick wall," but with the Skyray the culprit was trim drag, caused by the tuck-under phenomena in the transonic region.

By a curious twist of circumstances, the Skyray's "absolute" speed record lasted but a month, although its three kilometer mark remained unbroken for nearly eight years. As expected, within weeks of Verdin's flight, Lieutenant Colonel Frank Everest, Jr. piloted the YF-100 over the same Salton Sea course, exceeding the XF4D's record speed. Due to lower temperatures, however, Everest averaged only 757 mph. This was faster than the Skyray, but not by the required one percent for an official record.

Undaunted, North American officials took advantage of a little-known technicality in the F.A.I rules. It was discovered that the F.A.I. recognized the absolute speed record as the fastest average over either the three kilometer course at low altitude or the 15 kilometer at high altitude. A 15 kilometer course was hurriedly prepared at the Salton Sea, and Everest set a new 15 kilometer record of 755 mph. As this was faster than the Skyray's average, it was recognized as a new absolute speed record.

Remarkably, Verdin's three kilometer record at low altitude stood until August 28, 1961 when a Navy McDonnell F4H Phantom II flew 902.7 mph over a course set up at Holloman AFB, New Mexico but not without tragedy.

On the first attempt the airplane literally disintegrated at max speed because of a "JC" maneuver or PIO (pilot induced oscillation). I viewed the film of that accident, and it was the most horrible sight I ever saw, exceeding in terror the ball of fire which was the cockpit of a Navy fighter, containing the pilot, rolling up the flight deck after a ramp strike. The PIOs were clearly visible with G forces increasing with each cycle. After four cycles the plane just blew apart – engines, wings, tail, fuselage, cockpit and pilot were thrown in every direction.

Rocket vehicles have attained phenomenal velocities. For instance, the X-15, 4,250 mph; Apollo orbital velocity, 17,437 mph; Apollo Earth Escape Velocity, 24,496 mph. But when velocity is related to high dynamic pressure (indicated air speed) for powered aircraft capable of take-off and landing, the speed increase is only 13.6 mph/year during the seventy-five year history of powered aircraft. The first big increase in speed occurred in 1946 with the advent of the jet engine. Another small jump in the curve occurred when the afterburner came along in the early 1950s. The next *notch* will probably require a rocket engine with exotic materials for the airframe structure.

Since the XF4D was in a "racer" configuration, it seemed a waste not to try for the 100 kilometer, Closed-Course record, too. On Monday I approached Donald Douglas, Jr., with the idea. He raised no objection and suggested I look into the possibility of using the 100 kilometer course established by Jackie Cochran at Edwards. I flew to Edwards in a company Navion, obtained a map of the course from the Air Force and spent most of the morning spotting the pylons from the air.

Located at the north end of the Antelope Valley, the circular course was made up of 12 tall poles used as pylons. These were set equidistantly around Edwards AFB at 8.3 kilometer intervals (about 5.2 miles) for a total distance of 100 kilometers, or 62.1 miles. It encircled Rogers and Rosamond Dry Lake beds on the east and west sides, respectively. The whole area was made up of dry lake beds with shallow arroyos draining into them. It was sparsely populated except at its southern end where there were a few large turkey and chicken ranches. These were just northeast of the town of Lancaster and represented cause for concern as will be pointed out later.

After satisfying myself that the course was suitable, I telephoned Jackie at her ranch in Indio, California, to request permission to use it. She was in Japan at the time, but her husband, Floyd Odlum, told me the course was available to anyone.

Once again, Douglas requested permission from the Navy for the record attempt. The Navy was agreeable if it could be done with a minimum of delay to the Skyray testing program. It was assumed that a Navy flyer would be chosen to pilot the XF4D. Much to my surprise, however, a teletype was received from Bob Canaday, the Douglas-Navy liaison representative in Washington DC, stating that BuAer had approved me as pilot. The last line of his message read:

"Tell Rahn he owes me a beer."

I sent Canaday a *case* of beer posthaste to show my appreciation. As far as was known, this was the first and only time that a civilian was allowed to set a world record in an airplane owned by the US military.

We submitted another application to NAA and F.A.I. officials for the record try, which was nicknamed "Operation Merry-Go-Round."

I made several practice runs around the course in an F3D Skyknight during the next week, saving valuable engineering flight test time on the Skyray. On these flights I built up a mental log of landmarks surrounding each pylon as they were very difficult to spot at the high speeds and low altitudes at which the course had to be flown.

Finally satisfied with my "practice," I made one final flight over the course in the Skyray. During this run I had to secure my lap and shoulder belts as tightly as possible. Moving through the course at over 700 mph the XF4D was constantly shaken by rapid sharp jolts as it passed through the severe turbulence created by the heat thermals rising from the desert floor. I didn't want to crack my noggin on the canopy at such a fast rate of speed.

After completing only three-quarters of the course at high speed I cut the afterburner and ran the remainder of the flight in military power. I didn't want to "offend" the turkeys at the ranches at the southern end. We had heard that the noise of the afterburner and the Skyray's loud shock wave would literally scare the fowl to death.

I encountered no problems, so we decided to make an official try on Thursday, October 15th. To help spot the pylons a pile of old tires was stacked near each one and burned, allowing the ensuing dense, black smoke to mark the turns. In addition, two observers were stationed at each pylon; one to make sure that I stayed outside of the pole during the turn, the other to flash a small mirror at me which pinpointed the pylon.

The 15th turned out to be a relatively cool day as the temperature slowly peaked at only 76 degrees. As the many officials, timers and observers took their stations, the XF4D-1 was loaded with 640 gallons of fuel.

I started the Skyray's engine, did the checks, taxied into take-off position and was airborne within one minute and 20 seconds. I brought the XF4D up to 600 mph using military power as I executed a wide turn to the southwest. Then, while still several miles away from the first pylon, I lit the afterburner and jumped to maximum speed just as I reached the first pylon 100 feet above the ground. By F.A.I. rules I was restricted to a maximum altitude of 100 meters (about 300 feet), but I didn't want to fly higher than 100 feet and risk going inside the pylon.

I had no difficulty in negotiating the course. The day was beautifully clear. I easily located the smoke in the distance, then the mirror flashing and then the pylon itself. Continuing through the course my only real concern was maintaining speed through the turn. If I slowed too much as I pulled Gs in the turns, I could have "backed through" the Mach trim change. Had this happened, it would have caused increased control sensitivity and that would have induced a severe longitudinal control problem by inadvertent over controlling. It would have been a greater problem with higher temperatures, resulting in a lower Mach number, but the day was cool and I made the entire flight in the transonic speed range.

At least one newspaper account stated that I flew a circular path around the course in a constant 35 degree bank. Not so. The shortest distance between two points is a straight line. To minimize distance between pylons, therefore, I flew directly from one to the next, rounding each turn in a tight 70-degree bank. After each turn, which encompassed a heading change of 30 degrees, I rolled the Skyray back into level flight for the 15 seconds or so it took to reach the next pylon. I continued counterclockwise in this manner throughout the course without incident.

Overcoming initial reactions to the high speed, low altitude environment, I later reflected: "Flying at this speed so close to the ground, especially where longitudinal control is at its worst, was frightening at first, but after two-thirds of the attempt was over, I was reasonably relaxed and wished that I could get even more velocity. I actually found myself moving my upper torso fore and aft, urging the Skyray to go faster!"

The full circuit of the course took little more than five minutes. As I passed the last pylon, exhilarated, I hauled the Skyray up into a vertical climb and performed victory rolls on the way to 10,000 feet.

Upon landing I was congratulated by the Douglas crew and unofficial ground observers. They had timed the flight with stop watches, and after some quick calculations had determined that a new closed-course speed record had easily been set. The flight had lasted a little over ten minutes from take-off to landing, consuming roughly 600 gallons of fuel.

The Douglas team's rejoicing was cut short, however, as the NAA timers reluctantly notified the group that the official timing mechanism had malfunctioned, and that the attempt would not count.

We repeated the flight next day and, thankfully, duplicated the effort of the first. According to the same unofficial observers stopwatches, the second run was only .2 mph slower than the previous day's. The new official record was established by the Skyray at 728.11 mph. This beat the previous record of 709 mph by a substantial margin (set on September 19, 1953, by England's Neville Duke in a Hawker Hunter), and gave the 100 kilometer record back to the United States.

It was on this day that Bob Brush christened me "Rapid Robert." Every time we met over the next 40 years until his death, he called me that.

I have been asked why my circular course record was twenty-five mph slower than the three kilometer straight course record. There are four reasons: (1) higher altitude – 2,600 feet mean sea level, which reduced thrust; (2) lower temperature – twenty-two degrees, which resulted in lower true airspeed; (3) twelve, thirty degree turns were made, which reduced speed on each turn; and (4) flying *outside* of the pylon resulted in a distance greater than 100 kilometers.

Ironically, the record flight prompted an unexpected cost. The Douglas Aircraft Company received a bill for $1,800, the price of 450 turkeys who had been frightened to death by the Skyray's two full-afterburner circuits of the course. The same thing happened to Jackie Cochran during her record run of 652 mph in a Canadian built F-86 in May 1953. I wonder if there were any turkeys left for Thanksgiving that year!

The 100 kilometer record stood for over five years, but not because of any lack of aircraft capable of besting my speed. Rather, it was a combination of factors. There was growing dissatisfaction in the aviation community over the outdated F.A.I. rules which required the courses to be flown at dangerously low altitudes at speeds never imagined decades earlier. Performance-wise, these records had little bearing on a fighter's true capabilities as the turbojet was never intended to excel at low altitudes. Also, F.A.I.'s measurement in ground speed rather than Mach number didn't give a true picture of a modern fighter's performance.

In any event, as far as I know, my 100 kilometer closed course record was the last one set at low altitude. With sophisticated radar tracking and timing devices, all record attempts could now be flown at high altitudes where speed, as well as safety, could be achieved.

The record was eventually broken on February 25th, 1959, when Gerald Muselli piloted a Dassault Mirage III to 1,095 mph, at an altitude of 22,970 feet.

Not all of the Skyray's record breaking attempts were successful. In December 1953 the Navy was still basking in the spotlight of the XF4D's feats two months earlier. Influenced by that experience, the Navy decided to try for the world's altitude record of 63,668 feet which had been set the previous spring by a British Canberra bomber. This was easy to justify for the Navy because the Skyray was designed as an interceptor with quick climb capability.

The Navy also wanted to score a publicity coup by making
cial announcement of still another Skyray record at the Wright Brotl
morial Dinner slated for mid-December in the nation's capital. Vet
Verdin was assigned to make the try even though he had never fl
XF4D above 40,000 feet before. This placed substantial pressure on the Douglas support crew to come through again.

Trial flights began at Edwards with myself in the cockpit. My job in
what was called "Operation Flying Disc" was to prepare the engine for satisfactory operation at high altitude. The engine had operated perfectly throughout the high speed trials at low altitude but difficulties lay ahead.

I was checked out in an Air Force partial pressure suit because of the
extreme dangers to the human body in the event of loss of cabin pressure
above 45,000 feet. I even experienced explosive decompression in an altitude chamber at 80,000 feet (intentionally), which was far from a pleasant
experience.

At the outset, balky afterburner controls developed in the J-40 at high
altitude. I had compressor stalls – explosions, really – which occurred at a
rate of two per second. I experienced engine and duct rumbling. Then there
was engine backfiring, complete with sheets of flame that extended no less
than 10 feet out of the tailpipe. Plus, fuel starvation was causing afterburner
blow out – a real craw in our collective throat.

The main source of my anxiety had to do with complete engine failure and consequent loss of cabin pressurization. This would transform the
pressure suit into a vise, with me inside it. The windshield would frost up,
and I would have to go on the gauges. Trouble was, the aircraft wasn't instrumented for blind, or instrument flying. I carried ice scrapers so that I
could shave frost off the windshield.

We were working on problems right up to the morning of the day of
the banquet, December 18th. I was in the air with the afterburner lit, climbing but didn't have smooth operation of the AB and was not climbing satisfactorily. After I landed, the crew made one more small adjustment to the
fuel control in the hopes that Verdin could try for the record in the afternoon. Up to this time I hadn't been able to get the Skyray much over 50,000
feet.

Good as our intentions were, Jimmy could climb no further than
25,000 feet as the fuel control problems persisted. He was unable to even
light the afterburner.

At the banquet that night in Washington, DC no announcement of a
new altitude record was made, but Ed Heinemann was awarded the presti-
gious Collier Trophy by President Eisenhower for development of one of
America's first supersonic service fighters, the Skyray. He shared honors with
Dutch Kindelberger, who won for development of the F-100 Air Force fighter.
Dutch was the top man at North American Aviation and Ed had once worked
for him.

These were a dramatic and memorable three months for the Dou-
glas-El Segundo employees. In addition to the two world records and the
Collier Trophy Award, the D-558-2 Skyrocket scored an unofficial altitude
record of 83,235 feet with Marine Lieutenant Colonel Marion Carl at the controls, and NACA test pilot, Scott Crossfield, became the first man to fly twice
the speed of sound in the same airplane.

10

THE PRODUCTION JOB

I made the first flight in the production F4D with the J-57 installed in the summer of 1954. This 14,500 pound thrust power plant, with after-burning, improved the Skyray's performance significantly.

In addition to a different engine, the aircraft had a new flight control configuration with a different force-feel system, a different radar and a hinged canopy, so it was practically a different airplane altogether. The first flight was made out of Los Angles airport, and I was accompanied by an Air Force chase plane from Edwards.

Upon arriving over the Antelope Valley, my test flight was cut short due to a fire warning light. No way was I going to leap out of this airplane on its first flight because we had been waiting for this "production" job for a year. Therefore, I shut down the engine and began a dead stick approach. Since my chase pilot noticed no evidence of fire, and since the fire warning lights in those days were notorious for crying "Wolf!," I elected to restart the engine in the traffic pattern as a safety precaution. Above all, I didn't want to damage the airplane, so I elected to shut down again after the roll-out and was towed in. It was a good thing I took this precaution because inspection of the engine compartment showed that indeed, there had been a fire. At the time, we felt we were on a roll with this great fighter and proven engine. We felt that all of our problems were solved, but that was not to be.

The J-57 was a fine, reliable engine and that additional thrust over the J-40 engine enabled the Skyray to be a true interceptor. However, as with anything else, there is bad with the good. Due to its delta wing design and resultant low wing loading, the airplane was capable of pulling almost twice as many Gs at high altitude than present contemporary fighters. A compressor stall of the engine, however, almost always ensued, which negated the tactical advantage. We evaluated almost as many different engine duct inlets for the subsonic, high altitude, high alpha regime as we did tail cones for the high Mach, transonic speed range. We finally settled on the engine duct inlet design seen on production Skyrays.

We had a company rule that we had to wear pressure suits for flights at 50,000 feet and above. I was one of the first to use the Navy's full pressure suit in flight and in the F4D cockpit it was quite constricting. For this particular hop the purpose was to demonstrate maximum safe Mach Number starting from 50,000 feet.

I pushed over into a 45 degree dive and reached the design limit Mach of 1.5 at 35,000 feet. The test was successful as the demonstration point was attained, but I still had to recover. During the pullout, a partial structural failure of the left outboard elevon occurred. This caused an uncontrollable roll to the left. Upon recovery to level flight I discovered the engine had failed.

No sweat, or so I thought at the time. At 30,000 feet over the lake bed I extended the control stick and prepared for a dead stick landing, which turned out to be uneventful. I had to revert to manual flight control because the damaged elevon had failed the hydraulic control system. There was no thought of ejecting because that big, beautiful dry lake bed was near by, but thinking ahead about a possible ejection, in the event the damaged outboard elevon jammed, I tried to reach the overhead ejection handle. To my dismay, I found that I could not reach it because of the cumbersome and bulky, full pressure suit. Knowing that, I concentrated more intently upon making a successful landing, utilizing rudder for roll control, thus minimizing elevon deflection and a possible jam of the control.

Normally, after a dead sticker, the pilot goes to the Officers Club and has a few beers, but my problems were really just beginning. I couldn't get out of the cockpit by myself because of the damn pressure suit. It took twenty minutes for the ground support crew to reach me on the lake bed. I nearly died of heat prostration, sitting out in the direct desert sun before the ground crew got to me and helped me from the airplane.

It was at least 130 degrees in the cockpit. I guess that Fate didn't like the heat either as he must have departed and left me to myself.

To this day I would never wear a pressure suit while flying combat. I would want to be able to look at my six o'clock position without any constraints and be able to get out of the cockpit if necessary. Here again, not enough thought was given to the new flight environment. Before the next pressure suit flight, another ejection handle was rigged between the pilot's knees.

It was recently computed that this 45 degree dive to 1.5 Mach resulted in a descent rate of 62,000 feet per minute. This is considerably in excess of the former 90 degree dive in the AD of 44,000 feet per minutes. This didn't bother my ears at all because I was at a higher altitude where the air is thinner and the altitude loss was only 20,000 feet as compared with 28,000 feet for the AD.

One afternoon in 1955 over the Pacific in an F4D powered by the J-57, we were testing to determine if sufficient pitch trim was available to compensate for the tuck-under caused by compressibility at maximum level flight speed at sea level. Chuck Yeager was my chase pilot. Chuck is famous for being a good stick and rudder pilot and for flying close formation but he couldn't stay with me on this flight.

I had accelerated to Mach .98 (approximately 750 mph IAS at 100 feet above the water) in afterburner. This Mach speed created the maximum tuck-under. Full trimmer deflection was required to maintain trimmed flight. Trimmed flight means no pilot-force required on the control stick. Therefore I concluded that the engineers had done a good job with respect to adequate trim for this low altitude, high speed flight environment. For all practical purposes, the test was completed. So I nonchalantly shut off the afterburner.

Within 1.5 seconds the Skyray decelerated to subsonic speed which immediately increased trimmer effectiveness and eliminated the tuck-under. But the rapid deceleration – a fifty per cent loss in thrust – heaved me forward against the straps. There was no time to re-trim the airplane back to normal. My Skyray and I were pitched up at a gut wrenching 9.1 Gs. The airplane had a design limit of 7.0 Gs. Moreover, I wasn't wearing a g-suit. After all, this was only supposed to be a straight and level high speed run.

I immediately blacked out but was still able to think. I knew I was in a symmetrical pull-up, that I was climbing rapidly and losing airspeed just as fast. In order to reduce speed even faster I chopped the throttle to idle.

The fast deceleration of the plane would reduce the effectiveness of the trimmers, and the load factor would be lessened, thus allowing me to regain vision. I could then recover from whatever attitude in which I found myself, rather than splash into the ocean.

I didn't want to move the trimmers down because the switch was on the control stick, and I was fearful of inadvertently making a lateral input to the flight controls which might make matters worse. So I just flexed my stomach muscles in an effort to get the blood back into my head and rode it out.

After what seemed like an eternity I was able to see again, and what I saw was nothing but the blue Pacific. I was in a vertical dive after completing three-fourths of a loop. I forced myself to execute an extremely gentle recovery and when I got the machine level, at about 3,000 feet, I nervously examined the wings of my bird. They were wrinkled from wing tip to wing tip resembling dried prunes. I was in a ruined airplane, but one which was still flying.

Gently, heart half way up my throat, I nursed the jet back toward El Segundo, not knowing what internal failures might occur.

Chuck didn't know what had happened. In his vintage drawl he transmitted, "Bob, I lost you. Couldn't follow you in that maneuver. Where are you, over?"

I didn't know whether to laugh or cry and told him I was making an emergency landing at LAX. Chuck definitely broke the tension with his remark. I landed safely and noted afterward that the skin for the entire Skyray was wrinkled and some stringers in the dorsal fin were sticking through the skin. On top of that, the engine had broken away from its mounts and was laying on the engine compartment access door partially pinching a fuel line. How close I came to an engine failure, engine fire or complete structural failure I'll never know. The aircraft had to be scrapped.

Could what happened on that flight have been predicted? I had logged many sorties at 30,000 feet where the trimmers were deflected at transonic speeds to obtain data for the design of the trim change compensator, but the pitch-up when rapidly decelerating at high altitude was only 2.0 Gs. I had flown many times on the deck during the speed record runs, but the trimmers were not moved. Here were the clues. The speed runs were made at high temperature with the J-40 engine which had 40 percent less thrust, thus a lower Mach number and less tuck-under, plus the trimmers were not moved.

On this particular flight the temperature was colder over the ocean and with 40 percent more thrust, the airplane had accelerated to a higher Mach number than ever before on the deck. This Mach produced the peak tuck-under effect in the transonic region. Coupled with the maximum deflected trimmers, this set up the scenario for me. Old man Fate sat out there knowing it would happen. Luckily, I just barely slid away from his grasp, even under a blacked out condition, one more time.

This is the crux of present day flight testing. It isn't like the pre-World War II days with the test pilot and his silk scarf hell-bent for leather as portrayed in the movies. Days are spent analyzing data from the previous flight and planning the details for the next 30 minute hop. For this one we didn't do enough pre-flight thinking.

The flight recorder provided excellent data on the near mishap. It was remarkable how much damage was sustained and that the airplane was still flyable because it came within 1.4G of the *ultimate* design limit, a point at which the Skyray would theoretically break apart. The aircraft was a "strike" and not repairable, but we certainly learned a lot from it. Navy pilots were instructed *not* to trim the airplane in the transonic region at high indicated airspeed.

During one of the supersonic Mach dives I lost hydraulic pressure to the control system and had to revert to the emergency electric hydraulic system, which had limited control power for recovery. In the recovery the Skyray rolled uncontrollably to the left. Fortunately, it only rolled 60 degrees to the left before I was able to attain level flight. Then in level flight, there occurred a second failure. The nose pitched down abruptly indicating a malfunction in the control system. Engine oil pressure, became failure number three.

My immediate reaction was to get the Skyray back down on the ground as quickly as possible before engine seizure took place. Still, I had to analyze what was wrong with the control of the aircraft before diving to low altitude at high speed. Thus began a sequence of three cycles of diving and pulling out, working my way toward earth. I was in a hurry to get the airplane on the ground, but without excess airspeed.

This became a "roller coaster" emergency. After the third cycle, the chase pilot transmitted that my tail wheel was down. This probably meant that the nose down pitching moment was caused by the tail wheel extending into the air stream. That alleviated my concern about being able to control the aircraft.

The *fourth* failure occurred in the landing traffic pattern. I wasn't getting proper power response. Engine instruments indicated the variable exhaust nozzle was stuck in the full open position for afterburner operation. This minimized the amount of thrust available for the basic engine.

Finally, I landed and taxied up to the ramp where the crew chief excitedly signaled me to cut the engine because a fire had erupted in the engine section. This turned out to be a hydraulic fire, and the culprit was a leaking hydraulic line which caused the inadvertent extension of the tail wheel and the loss of hydraulic pressure for the flight control system.

Another task was to determine the safe jettison speed at various angles of attack for the fuel tanks mounted on pylons under the F4D's wings. This was required because a Skyray pilot on combat patrol might have to quickly get rid of his tanks to enhance maneuverability, rate of climb and maximum speed should he encounter enemy aircraft.

There was no trouble dropping the tanks at high speeds. Gradually, I worked down toward the slower speeds and with higher angles of attack. There might also be an occasion during an approach, for instance, when the pilot had to jettison the tanks because he was jumped by an enemy aircraft.

Everything appeared normal as the Skyray was cocked up in the landing attitude. I pickled the tank and to my shock and amazement the tank actually flew up and over the leading edge of the wing! When I returned to base and explained this phenomenon, we concluded that the tanks had developed sufficient lift to *fly* on their own. Thus they flew up and over the wing! The corrective solution was to avoid jettisoning tanks at slow, approach speeds.

We definitely had our share of close calls during experimental test flying of the Skyray in the 1950s. So many in fact that George Jansen coined the phrase, "Mayday, Skyray!" Still we always brought them back even though that one had to be scrapped because of the inadvertent 9.1 Gs. This was not the case with the Douglas production test pilots as they lost five aircraft over a short period of time and three of them were due to the failure of the so-called reliable J-57 engine. They were:

1. Pete Colepietro – loss of control, bail-out at speed near Mach 1.0
2. Walt Harper – engine failure, crash landing at Los Alamitos
3. Walt Harper – on his next flight: engine failure, bail-out
4. Chuck Kessler – engine failure, killed attempting dead stick landing at Los Alamitos
5. Raleigh Guynes – bailout from inadvertent spin

This high accident rate for production test flying was shocking to me. I would have had to bite my tongue if I were to repeat what I said to Jim Verdin a few years earlier when I told him that North American airplanes were dropping out of the skies like flies.

However, when the airplane was flown operationally by the Navy, it achieved a better than average accident rate for a high performance fighter.

The defining factor in the Skyray's design was its climbing ability. This was demonstrated for the first time during carrier qualification trials in 1953 aboard the *USS Coral Sea*. Jim Verdin flew the XF4D-1 to 40,000 feet in under five minutes, to meet the Navy's contract requirements.

Although the Skyray was designed to be a fast-climbing interceptor, its ability at this was never really pursued until 1955, more than four years after its first flight.

In the early months of 1955 a series of highly publicized, unofficial time-to-climb records was being established by various Navy aircraft. These flights were timed from brake release to 10,000 feet and presumably served to emphasize the Navy's increasing air might. In St. Louis, Missouri, McDonnell's F3H Demon, a Navy aircraft, posted the best time at 71 seconds in February.

We were conducting routine stability and control and performance flights at Edwards with the first production model of the F4D-1 with the J-57 installed. Late one Friday afternoon, a week after the Demon flight, Al Carder and I were sitting in his office at Edwards, discussing the next day's test schedule when the subject of the various time-to-climb flights came up. Somewhat puzzled, we both wondered what the other companies were trying to prove, since the Skyray, whatever its other failures, could surely take any climbing contest. After some discussion we decided to see what the Skyray could do the next day, "just for the hell of it," without any special preparation to the aircraft we were testing and, of course, without any practice.

At dawn, February 19th, I streaked down the runway at Edwards and pulled the F4D into a near-vertical climb, reaching 10,000 feet in just 56 seconds! In describing the event later I said, " My Ford Thunderbird, in accelerating up to 60 mph in 10 seconds, was terrific, but acceleration of the Skyray was astonishing, as I reached 160 mph in the same ten seconds. I was so busy during the remaining forty-six seconds after take-off trying to fly a prescribed airspeed and altitude schedule on instruments that I did not have time to react until the climb terminated. Looking back over my shoulder I saw the runway almost directly underneath me, 10,000 feet away. I was in a 70 degree angle climb traveling at the climb rate of 28,000 feet per minute."

Though it was widely publicized, the flight was unofficial. And though it was obvious in 1955 that the Skyray could have easily broken the existing world time-to-climb records, an official attempt was not made for three more years. Then, in February 1958, Douglas submitted a proposal to BuAer's Fighter Branch, requesting that an F4D-1 make an attempt at besting the four French-held records of 3,000, 6,000, 9,000 and 12,000 meters. These had been set a year earlier by Michael Chalard in a Nord 1405 Gerfaut 88 at Istre, France. Douglas engineering data indicated the Skyray could take the records by a substantial margin. They also hoped to set an entirely new record of 15,000 meters, nearly 50,000 feet.

Although BuAer had also received a "feeler" from Vought and their F8U-1 Crusader, it was evidently decided the Skyray stood a better chance to break the French marks and Douglas received permission to proceed with the attempt.

Chief of the Bureau at the time was Rear Admiral Robert Dixon and he authorized funds for the effort, dubbed "Operation Intercept." The admiral designated Edward N. LeFaivre, a thirty-seven year old Marine major, to pilot the F4D-1 in the attempts. He was the Project Pilot for the aircraft. I was assigned as Deputy Director of the time-to-climb record attempts. Bob Goedhart was assigned as Director.*

The NAA was notified and asked to supply the necessary supporting/official cast. As with the Skyray's previous record attempts, these officials would certify the times and forward the results, accordingly, to the F.A.I. in Paris for final certification and recognition.

On Monday the 12th of May, LeFaivre met with Douglas personnel in Los Angeles to discuss the techniques to be used during the trial flights. There were many problems in logistics and in plotting the correct flight profile for each altitude attempt. What climb angle would be used? What was the maximum allowable engine temperature? How much G force should be applied during rotation? What measuring and recording instruments would be required?

The sixth production aircraft was assigned for the flight. It was owned by the Navy but technically on bailment to Douglas because of the continuing need for test work, plus the high cost that would be required to rework it to operational configuration. Contrary to publicity releases, the aircraft was far from being strictly a standard production model. Various items had been removed to lighten the aircraft, including the four 20 millimeter cannons, wing and belly stores and pylons, certain electronics, and the tailhook and tail wheel assembly. Special test instrumentation was carried, including a long, tapered pitot tube boom on the nose that projected ahead of the Skyray's shock wave to give more accurate readings.

New Wasp-alloy turbine blades were installed on the J-57-P8 engines, allowing higher engine operating temperatures which permitted an increase in the afterburning thrust of the normal P8's 14,500 pounds.

It was decided to make the record attempt at the Naval Air Missile Test Center, Point Mugu, California, an air base situated 50 miles northwest of Los Angeles along the coast. Here, the cold dense sea air would enable the engine to operate at its maximum thrust to provide the maximum rate of climb. Prevailing onshore winds would also help reduce the Skyray's take-off roll.

We made practice flights at Edwards in mid-May with LeFaivre flying nine separate trial hops to test the aircraft's performance with the modified engine to practice some spin recoveries, and to familiarize himself with the different flight profiles during the rapid full instrument climbs.

Each separate altitude try called for a slightly different flight profile. The technique for the 3,000 meter mark was simple enough: lift off at 150 knots, pull 1.4 Gs until a 70 degree attitude was attained, then zoom to 3,000 meters, holding the 70 degree climb attitude. But for each succeeding height, the flight profile became more complicated as the Skyray's climbing ability varied with altitude.

The 15,000 meter profile, for example, was especially troublesome. After lifting off, it was necessary to accelerate to Mach .9 up to 10,000 feet. LeFaivre then had to maintain a specified Mach number (about .79) in a climb to 40,000 feet. At this altitude the aircraft was zoomed, pulling up at about 1.5 Gs until 50,000 feet was reached. What made the flight especially uncomfortable for LeFaivre was the fact that a 10 to 15 degree engine overtemp occurred on each flight above 35,000 feet. Furthermore, at 43,000 feet the afterburner flamed out, followed shortly by a basic engine flameout at 46,000 feet. After this happened, LeFaivre held his zoom attitude of 60 degrees until he reached 50,000 feet. At that height his airspeed was around 70 knots and he let the airplane fall forward in a dive to 25,000 feet, where he restarted the engine.

During these practice flights the combination of desert heat and altitude at Edwards caused the initial thrust and acceleration of the Skyray to suffer a bit. Because of this, the times recorded for the various flights were greater than those needed to break the records, but this caused no real concern to LeFaivre or the Douglas crew.

LeFaivre flew the Skyray to Point Mugu on Monday, May 19th, and preparations were made for the official flights. That afternoon, and during the next two days, LeFaivre practiced each climb once more, except for the troublesome 15,000 meter climb, which he tried three more times. The effect the denser sea air had on thrust and acceleration was fantastic, and during the initial practice flights at Point Mugu, a major problem developed because of this. Due to the rapid acceleration of the aircraft, the hydraulically actuated landing gear doors would not close. LeFaivre tried three times to start the retraction cycle the instant the aircraft left the ground, but in each case the doors were torn by the air stream. Fortunately, the problem was solved by simply increasing the hydraulic system operating pressure. This closed the doors several seconds earlier. End of problem.

Late Wednesday, the 21st, LeFaivre and the project crew were ready to begin the measured record attempts, and preparations were made to start the following morning. Bert Rhine and Dr. W.S. Dixon, official representatives of NAA had jurisdiction over the flights and the special clocking instrumentation. Radar tracking devices would verify the altitudes achieved and the timing clocks would be started as LeFaivre initiated a countdown over the radio.

Taking advantage of the cold morning air, LeFaivre made the first attempt, to 3,000 meters, at dawn. With minimum fuel in his tanks, he taxied to a starting line marked on the runway and ran the engine to full speed while checking the instruments for proper readings. Ten seconds away from brake release he began the countdown. At zero he released the brakes, engaged the afterburner, and thundered down the runway, gaining momentum rapidly. At the same instant, cameras began recording the climb and the tracking radar was triggered.

As the full afterburning thrust took effect, LeFaivre felt the tremendous acceleration of the lightened Skyray. In only a few seconds the F4D-1 reached 150 knots and LeFaivre pulled the Skyray into a near-vertical climb. The airplane literally stood on a tail of flame as it streaked to 3,000 meters in 44.39 seconds, bettering the French mark by nearly seven seconds.

LeFaivre landed a few minutes later, having used only 400 pounds of fuel during the flight. There were congratulations, refueling, and preparation for the 6,000 meter attempt.

Similar procedures were used for the remaining flights with LeFaivre taxiing to the starting line, counting down, and kicking in the afterburner as he let go the brakes.

He also broke the 6,000 and 9,000 meter time to climb records that day. The Skyray reached the first mark in 1:06:13 minutes, and the second was broken in 1:29:81 minutes, both substantially beating the French efforts.

The final two altitude tries were saved for next morning. LeFaivre set the 12,000 meter record with a 1:51:23 run. The final 15,000 meter flight was also successful, establishing an entirely new time-to-climb record for the altitude at 2:36:05.

Upon recognition of these marks by the F.A.I., the Skyray held a total of seven world records, although briefly. By 1958, time and progress rapidly caught up to the F4D-1, not to mention the disgust of the USAF which naturally felt that all records should have been the exclusive property of Air Force fighters.

In less than seven months the Air Force captured all of these time-to-climb records with their new F-104A. In December 1958 Lieutenant Einar Enevoldson of the Air Force set new records for the 3,000 and 15,000 meter events. Lieutenant William Smith also broke the 6,000, 9,000 and 12,000 meter marks.

Following are some of the lessons learned over 40 years ago while testing radical supersonic fighters:

1. Emergency manual flight controls are not satisfactory. A redundant power system is a must and a fail operational/fail safe system should be considered.

Above: Bob Rahn, in the Douglas Skyray, enters the 100 km closed-course at Edwards AFB.

Below: He flashes across the finish line establishing a new record of 728.11 mph. (Douglas)

Bob Rahn strapped into the Douglas Skyray just prior to the 100 km closed course record flight. (Douglas)

Various Douglas wing forms are exhibited in this photo taken at Edwards AFB.
Clockwise from the bottom are the XF4D delta wing; the Skystreak with transonic wing;
the thin wing supersonic X-3; and the Skyrocket, first to attain Mach 2.0. (Douglas)

Above: A gathering of aviation notables at the El Segundo Management Club Annual Navy Night: (l. to r.) Bill Bridgeman, Don Douglas, Jr., Eric Springer (first Douglas test pilot), Lt. Cdr. Jim Verdin, and Bob Rahn. (Douglas)

Below: Jim Verdin and Bob Rahn receive awards from a resentative of the F.A.I. at the Wright Brothers Banquet in Washington, DC Dec. 1953. (Douglas)

Donald Douglas, Jr. presents Bob Rahn with a model of the XF4D Skyray. (Douglas)

Rahn streaking to 10,000 feet in the Skyray during an unofficial time-to-climb record attempt.

Maj. Ed LeFaivre, holder of five time-to-climb records achieved in the Douglas Skyray. (Douglas)

First flight of the Douglas XA4D Skyhawk, June 1954. (Mc Donnell Douglas, Harry Gann)

Above: Experimental test pilots for the Skyhawk confer: (l. to r.) George Jansen, Bob Rahn, Bill Bridgeman and Jim Verdin. (Douglas)
Below: The unique tail assembly of the Skyhawk is shown in this simulator. (Douglas)

"Tadpole" Rudder

Left: This head-on view of the Skyhawk shows off its long, narrow landing gear. (Douglas)

Below: The support crew, all of whom had a hand in the Skyhawk's record 500 km closed course record. Bob Rahn is seated to the left of the sign and pilot, Lt. Gordon Gray is right of the sign. (Douglas)

THIS A4D-I HAS JUST BROKEN THE 00 KILOMETER WORLDS SPEED RECORD OCT 15,1955

The last of 2,960 production Skyhawks is adorned with the flags of seven nations that utilized the plane. It is armed with Maverick missiles and carries the colors of a Marine attack squadron. (USN)

On rollout the Skylancer looked like it had clipped wings and winglets. But this folded wing configuration was meant to accomodate carrier operations. (Douglas)

Bob Rahn takes a nap in the cockpit of the Douglas XF5D Skylancer as he awaits an Air Force chase plane for the first flight of the supersonic beauty that he termed the "Cadillac." It was April 21, 1956 at Edwards AFB. (Douglas)

The F5D snapped in supersonic flight. (McDonell-Douglas, Harry Gann)

A group of aviators at the Happy Bottom Riding Club with the famous Pancho Barnes, top row second from the right. (Harry Clayton)

The Douglas A3D-2 Skywarrior. (Mc Donnell Douglas, Harry Gann)

This Skywarrior lived up to its name and landed itself after the crew parachuted. (USAF)

Ed Heinemann, Douglas'
legendary chief engineer
and Bob Rahn. (Douglas)

Douglas' first test pilot, Eric Springer (far right), receives an honorary fellowship in SETP.
Left to right are Mr. and Mrs. Donald Douglas, Jr. and Bob Rahn.

Bob Rahn in 1969 during his tenure as Apollo Test and Operations Research Pilot, responsible for check-out of the Apollo 11, Command Module. (North American Rockwell)

Bob Rahn flying the tethered prototype lunar flyer while wearing a full NASA pressure suit. (Rockwell)

Space shuttle *Columbia* glides to a landing at Edwards AFB on April 14, 1981. (Rockwell Int.)

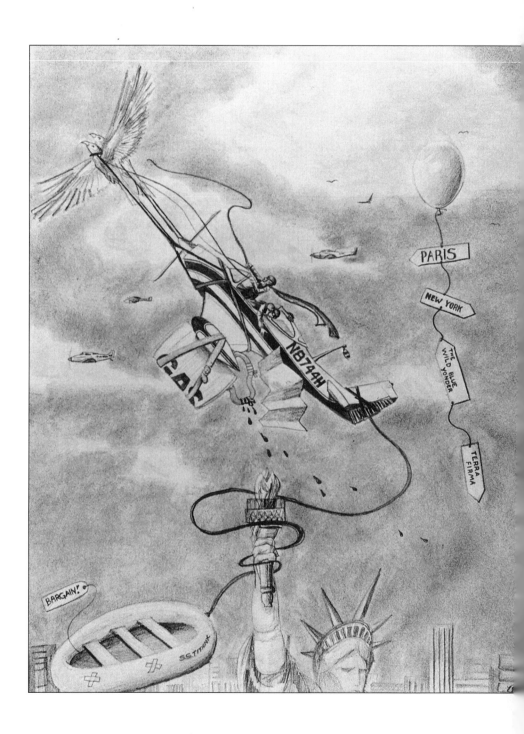

Rahn's nephew created this cartoon to "honor" Uncle Bob's Dayton/New York/Paris flight in the Navion.

With his wife, Feppy, and his Navion Bob Rahn continues to fly. The flags represent countries visited.

Seated in a museum Spitfire Bob Rahn has made a 50-year full circle with this photo taken in England during a 31st Fighter Group reunion.

ROBERT O. RAHN
CAPTAIN USAAF
DOUGLAS AIRCRAFT COMPANY
1920-

AFTER 103 WWII COMBAT MISSIONS FLYING SPITFIRES IN THE
EUROPEAN THEATRE, ROBERT "BOB" RAHN GRADUATED FROM THE
USAAF'S 2ND TEST PILOT CLASS AND BECAME AN EXPERIMENTAL
TEST PILOT AT WRIGHT FIELD.

IN LATE 1945 RAHN JOINED DOUGLAS (LATER McDONNELL DOUGLAS)
AS AN ENGINEERING TEST PILOT, AND OVER THE NEXT 11 YEARS DID
THE FIRST FLIGHT, DEVELOPMENT, SPIN, ETC. TESTS ON A NUMBER
OF PLANES INCLUDING THE:

AD SKYRAIDER ATTACK BOMBER SERIES
F4D SKYRAY INTERCEPTOR SERIES
A4D SKYHAWK LIGHT ATTACK BOMBER

TESTING THE SKYRAIDERS, 1945-49, RAHN SET AN UNOFFICIAL WORLD
RECORD FOR PAYLOAD (BOMBS, ROCKETS, ETC.) AT 10,000 LBS.

IN 1953 THE SKYRAY PILOTED BY BOB BECAME THE FIRST CARRIER
AIRCRAFT CAPABLE OF MACH 1.0 IN LEVEL FLIGHT AND TO HOLD
A WORLD SPEED RECORD.

AD SKYRAIDER
CARRIER BASED 1946-1969

F4D SKYRAY
CARRIER BASED 1956-1963

Bob Rahn's aviation accomplishments are immortalized in this plaque aboard
the *Lexington* Museum at Charleston, SC.

2. Pilots don't like to make large rudder inputs to coordinate a turn, so adverse yaw with roll must be corrected by other means.

3. The use of telemetry is a must for safer and more rapid advances while exploring the unknown regions of an airplane's flight envelope.

4. Small increases in IAS or Mach number can create disastrous results. Always anticipate problems and prepare to use emergency procedures.

5. Wear your protective clothing. If a G suit had been worn during the inadvertent pitch-up, the anxiety would have been considerably reduced.

6. Use a "hot" mike to describe in real time the characteristics of a spin.

7. Perform inverted spins as soon as possible after the initiation of a spin program.

For three years the Skyray was a most interesting and exciting program to be associated with, but I was looking forward to being assigned to a new airplane being built at El Segundo with an entirely new design concept.

* Ironically, Bob and his wife were later killed in a ground collision of two Boeing 747s in the Canary Islands in an accident which took the lives of more than 500 people.

11

HEINEMANN'S HOT ROD

The Spitfire I flew in World War II was a great success largely because it was a light aircraft of uncomplicated design with no frills. That experience was the main factor that induced me to become a test pilot. I wanted to help the U.S. develop effective, lightweight, fighters of simple design. The A-4 (A4D) Skyhawk was not a fighter but it embodied the fundamental simplicity which was Ed Heinemann's trademark. There was great satisfaction in testing this wonderful flying machine.

In the early 1950s the Navy specification for a jet propelled attack aircraft to replace the workhorse Skyraider called for a design with a maximum gross weight of 30,000 pounds. Heinemann excited, if not shocked, the Navy by asserting he could produce an airplane that would exceed the desired design speed by ninety knots and weigh only half as much!

The original contract, written in June 1952, called for construction of a single prototype aircraft because many officials in the Navy were skeptical that such a "diminutive" warplane could be built. Additionally, the Navy could not pay more than one million dollars for the aircraft, an astonishingly small figure in today's aviation market place.

Because the design concept was comparatively small in size, a full-scale mockup was built to ensure that everything would fit into the compact environment The cockpit accommodated my six foot, 190 pound frame but there was little room to spare. The ejection seat apparatus included a parachute built into the system. The pilot restraint, parachute harness, and g-suit were integrated into a single garment. This flying suit was designed specifically for the XA4D and allowed the parachute to remain with the airplane.

The Skyhawk was rolled out at a gross weight of 14,600 pounds. Its empty weight was a remarkable 8,136 pounds. It was powered by the British Sapphire J-65 engine built by Curtiss Wright and capable of producing 7,200 pounds of thrust. Wing span was only twenty-seven and one-half feet, a factor that eliminated the need for wing-folding aboard the carrier. Construction of the wing included three, single piece spars with single sheets of skin from tip to tip.

The windshield was a single piece, lightweight design. The wing slats operated aerodynamically, the rudder was manual, the elevator was boosted, and the ailerons had a single, hydraulically powered system with a manual system back-up. The control stick could be extended to provide mechanical advantage in the event of a hydraulic system failure.

At a private meeting in Ed Heinemann's office I told him I was in full accord with his concept, and would not write up any specific deficiency in test reports if it didn't meet the specifications, but would just describe what the airplane did. The exceptions were: (a) safety of flight items and; (b) if it could not perform the specified mission. We agreed to keep an open mind and to present the marginal items to the NPE Test Team for their evaluation.

An example of this is a specification that calls for the capability to lift the nose wheel off the ground on take-off at 90 percent stall speed. I couldn't do it even with full aft stick, but it did lift off at stall speed. I found that by holding full forward stick during the take-off roll and then yanking back at 90 percent stall speed, the specification could be met. This was because the long nose wheel strut was fully compressed with the stick forward, and when it was released, the dynamic effect helped to lift the nose wheel off the ground.

Of course, this is a stupid way to fly an airplane during take-off. On the other hand, it would have been even more stupid to add more weight and complexity by building a larger elevator or allowing more up travel since the present one was satisfactory for all other regions of flight. Thousands of A-4s have been flying for forty years with no one complaining about this deficiency.

"Heinemann's Hot Rod" was dubbed with many other nicknames over the years: Tin Can, Bantam Bomber, Scooter, and Tinker Toy, among them. It looks aerodynamically clean, but this is not necessarily the case. Many protuberances were added to improve its aerodynamic characteristics during the developmental tests of the aircraft.

That first flight ended uneventfully. The only "squawk," or discrepancy, came at the first-flight party in Palmdale where, after a half dozen martinis, I proclaimed loud and unclear, "Wash we need ish more thrush." A short time later Wright provided an additional 500 pounds of thrust in the J-65.

While flying through slightly turbulent air at 300 knots during the third flight, there occurred an irregular torsional movement of the empennage which caused a snaking-flight profile. Aft fuselage stiffeners were attached to prevent the empennage from twisting.

I also experienced buffet emitting from the tail at high indicated speed. We experimented with five different tail cone fairings before a simple, inverted sugar scoop cleaned up the airflow between the tail pipe and the horizontal stabilizer.

The test program progressed smoothly during the first nine months. We had nearly completed Part I of the aerodynamic and structural demonstration, and the flight envelope had been explored up to almost 600 knots. Returning to base after completing a routine test one day, I flew under a cumulus cloud at about 10,000 altitude and 450 knots. All of a sudden, the Skyhawk seemed as if it were coming apart. There was a violent rudder flutter, induced by the turbulence from the cloud. I immediately came "back, out or on" with everything: throttle, elevator, speed brakes, and instrumentation to slow the airplane down and gather data. The Skyhawk was shaking so fiercely I had difficulty finding the instrumentation switch to turn it on. After a moment I was out of it and made a normal landing.

There was little damage to the airplane and the rudder and fin were still in one piece. The oscillograph records indicated rudder flutter with a total amplitude of 12 degrees at 14 cycles per second and the fin tip had a total excursion of 12 inches.

I was reluctant to proceed with the flutter program because I was both physically and mentally shaken by the flutter that had occurred inadvertently at a speed much lower than had been flown before. This was the kind of mystery that put me ill at ease. I could sense the onset of fear. Why had it happened? We had checked for flutter throughout the speed range. We had to go back to the drawing board.

A dashpot, which functioned as a kind of shock absorber, was added to the control linkage to combat the flutter, and telemetry was installed to provide real-time data to pacify my anxiety. I had difficulty duplicating the flutter, however, eventually achieving it by kicking the rudder pedal as sharply as possible at the desired airspeed.

Over the next several months we tried many different configurations to correct the flutter. What finally did the trick was a "tadpole rudder". The tadpole was nothing more than a flat plate of skin with the ribs mounted externally, reducing the vortices around the aft chord of the rudder. It performed magnificently with a damping ratio of better than three percent. However, we had to credit North American engineers as the tadpole design was "borrowed" from their FJ-3 Fury aircraft.

It was rumored that Douglas had to pay a small royalty fee to North American for the use of this design for each production airplane. Though insignificant, Kindelberger must have enjoyed having this one-upmanship for the next twenty-six years.

Bob (R.B.) Smith was at it again. His calculations showed that the Skyhawk, with only internal fuel, could break the 500 kilometer closed course World Speed Record. So, we decided to make some speed runs in the aircraft. I made a number of preliminary circuits around the 100 kilometer course at Edwards AFB to see if the Skyhawk would hold together, especially considering the severe turbulence likely to be encountered over the desert floor. I also wanted to determine what speed might be expected, and if there was sufficient internal fuel to make a try at the 500 kilometer closed course record. The development flights were made with trailing edge bulb rudder (a design modification which corrected the flutter problem but resultd in high rudder forces). Flying over 600 knots (695 mph), 100 feet above the ground over the hot desert, is not a comforting experience. Make an error down that low and that fast and your life could be over in a microsecond.

However, after the first circuit around the course at max speed, I was unaware of any unusual characteristics during the flight, except that it was quite turbulent. As I taxied back to the ramp, though, onlookers were pointing to the tail. Close examination revealed a tear in the aft fuselage skin about the size of a football, a few wrinkles in the nose cone, and the top aft portion of the rudder (about six inches by six inches) was missing.

Since it was late in the year, the temperature was dropping, the official timers were ready and there was little schedule time left, we decided to change to the tadpole design instead of repairing the other rudder, which required an additional rib. To eliminate the risk of losing the same piece on the tip of the tadpole, we cut a section out to resemble that portion lost. Then we "sewed" the rudder back up again.

Lieutenant Gordon Gray set a new world record in the Skyhawk of 695.163 mph on the very first attempt in 1955, on internal fuel. This eclipsed the mark held by an F-86H which used a drop tank. Not bad for an attack airplane. Incidentally, this was the only time that an attack airplane has held this record.

Before the official flight, anybody who wanted to could estimate what the official speed would be and put a dollar in the kitty. The crew chief on the aircraft won the pot – a hundred thirty dollars. That proves that some of the mechanics know more about their airplane than the pilots or the engineers. My estimate was several mph slower than that attained. Gordie did a good flying job for five circuits of the course.

The Skyhawk was not designed for making supersonic dive bombing attacks, yet it was possible to fly supersonically in the XA4D using military thrust and diving at 30 degrees. The hydraulically boosted elevator, however, did not provide much pullout capability. At the time, this did not appear to be a disqualifying factor because there was no requirement to deliver an external store at supersonic speed. It was not until the aerodynamic demonstration for maximum safe Mach number was made that it became apparent we had, so to speak, a Skyhawk by the tail.

Flight rules were formulated to describe the normal technique that a fleet pilot would instinctively use in recovering from a maximum Mach number dive They were:

1. One hand on the stick with 120-pound pull force
2. No horizontal stabilizer retrim
3. Retard throttle to idle
4. Open speed brakes

I could have used other specialized techniques, such as judiciously employing electric stabilizer trim, extending the stick to increase mechanical advantage, and pulling 200 pounds of force with both hands, but we believed that these actions were above and beyond the call of duty for the average service pilot. I didn't want to have to use the stabilizer because of the severe pitch-up problem I had experienced with the F4D when the pitch trimmers were used in the transonic region.

Work-up flights were conducted at 30, 45 and 60 degree dive angles for the purpose of familiarizing myself with the characteristics of the airplane. The final demonstration dive was started by attaining maximum speed at 45,000 feet with military thrust and then pushing over to a 70 degree dive angle using the zero lift technique.

As in any high speed dive, when approaching the design limits of the airplane, I was extremely busy scanning the instrument panel, my eyes constantly checking on the attitude gyro, the Mach meter, and the altimeter. I initiated pull-out at 30,000 feet and achieved recovery to level flight at 12,000 feet. There was no buffet, flutter, or uncontrollability of the airplane at 1.2 Mach which also was the maximum structural limit at high altitude. What defined this as being the maximum safe Mach Number point was that it required 18,000 feet to recover. I could only pull 1.8 G with 120 pounds of stick force until the airplane decelerated subsonically.

I felt like the proverbial cowboy going over a cliff on his horse, shouting, "Whoa, whoa, you son of a gun!" A powered elevator on the -2 model of the A4D solved this problem and made the airplane considerably safer for the service pilot. By trimming her with a push force at supersonic speed, another test pilot "Knick" Knickerbocker was able to pull 7.0 Gs at approximately 1.1 Mach.

The total altitude lost during the dive and recovery was 33,000 feet and was considerably in excess of the total altitude excursion on the AD structural demonstration dive of 27,800 feet, of which 7,800 feet were used for the pull-out.

With the AD in the first 90 degree dive performed, compressibility effect on the elevator was totally unexpected. Whereas with the A-4, I knew beforehand that I had a Skyhawk by the tail, because the previous "build-up" dives resulted in low G pull-outs with the boosted elevator, but I knew I could control it if I had enough altitude.

As a back up, I had planned before the demonstration dive that if still supersonic at 10,000 feet I would extend the stick to increase mechanical advantage and judiciously "tweak" the stabilizer.

I thought that my rate of descent on the 90 degree dive in the AD-1 was outstanding, but on this dive in the A4D it was incredible how fast the altimeter was unwinding. The needle of the sensitive altimeter was a blur. It was calculated that the maximum rate of descent was 67,000 feet per minute. At this rate, it would have taken only 27 seconds from 30,000 feet to fall and splatter all over the landscape. Quite a contrast to an unpressurized airliner's normal rate of descent of only 500 feet per minute.

Fate, the hunter, was busy stalking someone else because he knew that with our planning, preparation, work-up flights – and back up capabilities – he would be wasting his time looking for me.

It used to be that only two turns were required, with no inverted entries, for the formal spin demonstration for an attack airplane. This was a carry-over from the concept that an attack designation implied it was a big airplane and was not required to perform unusual maneuvers like a fighter plane. The original thinking was that there was no tactical reason for this type of vehicle to inadvertently get into an inverted spin so none were investigated, although spins were performed both to the left and to the right in many other different types of entries. These were as follows:

1. Symmetrical stall – power off and with normal-rated thrust (NRT) in the clean configuration
2. One-third aileron held with the spin
3. One-third aileron against the spin
4. 2.5G accelerated stall turn
5. Landing configuration – power off and with NRT

As to spin tests in the A4D, the accelerated turn entry was the most uncomfortable to execute. In a right turn entry around 200 knots, pulling a 2.6G to attain an accelerated stall in the clean configuration at 40,0000 feet at normal-rated thrust, the first turn usually entailed a snap roll upon application of full rudder. This degenerated into a highly oscillatory spin in roll and yaw. Pitch oscillation usually diminished to a near vertical attitude by one and one-half turns and was accompanied by intense buffeting of the whole airplane because the indicated airspeed remained high. The spin rate varied from slow to fast because of the extreme oscillation in roll and yaw, which was of sufficient magnitude to cause three temporary reversals in spin direction to the left, even while holding full right pro-spin controls. A considerable loss in altitude occurred during this type of entry and recovery because of the near-vertical attitude and relatively high air speed. However, recovery was very positive in a one-quarter turn, which usually required just the use of neutral controls.

For the other type entries, the rudder was very effective in the Skyhawk. The airplane entered the spin promptly. Spin characteristics included fast auto-rotation for one-half turn followed by a slow rate accompanied by irregular oscillations about all three axis. Since I only had to make two turns in the spin, the spin never fully developed. Recovery never required more than one-half turn and it was accomplished using the standard procedure of opposite rudder and neutral elevator. In fact, the recovery was so straightforward with minimum loss of altitude (except for the accelerated stall) that I completed the entire formal demonstration of fourteen spins on a single flight.

Configuration and aft center of gravity are two key parameters in determining the spin and recovery characteristics of an airplane. Let me describe how different an accelerated 2.5 G entry in the TA-4, twin-seat version of the Skyhawk was in a clean configuration. Fortunately for me, Knick Knickerbocker, was involved in this program.

At 40,000 feet, he applied full right rudder and full aft stick for the accelerated entry. The Skyhawk snap rolled into what became a horizontal spin. After a few irregular gyrations it rolled upside down and went into an *inverted* spin with Knick holding full pro-controls for an upright spin. Initially, the inverted spin characteristics were very erratic. The significant changes in pitch had to be disorienting for Knick. When the airplane was upright, he thought he was in an upright spin, so he applied normal recovery controls. But doing that only aggravated the situation. This also was his first inverted spin and, unfortunately, it was also inadvertent or unintended.

As the inverted spin progressed, the pitch and roll excursions diminished with each turn. After ten turns it was like a model test in a spin tunnel. It was fully developed now, with a steady rotation of approximately three seconds per turn and small oscillations in pitch and roll.

One corollary is that if an aircraft is difficult to spin, recovery will be easy. If its easy to spin, recovery is difficult.

Knick's spin should be submitted to the Guinness Book of World Records for the highest number of inverted turns completed before recovering – an astonishing thirty-three turns! I don't think anyone can beat that and to my knowledge no one ever has.

I have often wondered how many turns I made during the inadvertent inverted spin in the Skyray, but since we did not have the long range ground camera at Edwards at the time, I'll never know. Anyway, I wouldn't qualify for the Guinness Record Book because mine was not a normal recovery – I used the spin chute.

Lateral stability tests went well in the Skyhawk. About a year later, however, during a one-minute, steady heading sideslip at slow speed, near the end of a flight, I experienced negative lateral stability. This meant the airplane was rolling in one direction while I held the control column in the opposite, a potentially dangerous situation.

At a post-flight meeting everyone was baffled as to the cause. The next flight card was made out with this test at the top of the list, except the problem had gone away. The airplane was inherently stable. Bewildering! Subsequent test flights were even more confusing. Sometimes the tests were negative, sometimes positive. Other times, near the end of the flight, the amount of negative stability became worse the longer the sideslip was held.

We debated the issue ceaselessly for a few days. Finally, we realized the problem: there were NO BAFFLES in the single integral wing tank. The negative lateral stability was caused by fuel flowing to the low wing during long steady sideslips. The worst case of negative stability occurred when the wing was half full of fuel. This situation was unsatisfactory and was fixed by the installation of baffles in the production airplane.

One episode in my Skyhawk experience does not make me smile with fondness, because I had a run-in with the Federal Bureau of Investigation. After completing the spin demonstration at Pax the Hertz rental car was returned to a downtown office in Washington DC. I inadvertently left a confidential copy of the A4D Pilot's Operating Instructions, or handbook, in the trunk of the Chevrolet, and the Hertz people discovered it.

Instead of notifying me at my hotel, or contacting the Douglas office in Washington, Hertz personnel went directly to the FBI. On arrival at the Santa Monica plant in California, two FBI agents were waiting for me.

They told me that I was under investigation because of the handbook. Consequently, I was denied access to confidential or secret data. The FBI allowed me to report to work each day, but they isolated me from all employees, like a kid stuck in the corner with a dunce hat on his head. I was banished to a storage room out by the flight office during working hours for the next thirty days.

I was allowed limited flying but for the most part spent hour after hour by myself in that storage room. The FBI would not allow me to visit the spaces where I normally would go – where the handbook and other related documents of the trade were stored. Some of my time was spent writing up my evaluation of the Grumman F11F which I had flown while on the East Coast. The FBI wouldn't even let me proof read my own typewritten report.

Donald Douglas Jr., Vice President of the company and head of the Test Division at the time, went to bat for me writing a very strong letter to the FBI explaining how important I was to the company and to the nation in testing the Skyhawk. No one else was qualified to take my place, he told them, and my absence was holding up the program. He went into detail about my background and made a fervent case on my behalf, so good that had the circumstances been different, I would have asked Don for a raise right there on the spot.

Nothing could be done to expedite the investigation, however. Toward the end of my exile, I was in Don's office when he received a call from the FBI. From the tone of the conversation it was "iffy" whether I would get my secret clearance back.

"What do you want, a quart of blood?" Don said loudly and with great frustration into the phone.

Finally, at the end of the thirty days, the restriction was lifted, and I was allowed to return to full scale duty. It took a while to get over this unhappy interlude which could have ended my test flying career very abruptly.

The XA4D could enter the transonic region easily, by nosing over into a 10-degree dive angle at high speed. The airframe would experience light buffet and small pitch down, but the disqualifying feature of the prototype was an erratic and abrupt wing drop either to the right or left of about 30 degrees. We tried eleven different vortex generator patterns before we settled on an arrangement featuring one row on the leading edge slat and one row just in front of the aileron.

A vortex generator in the configuration for the Skyhawk was a small piece of aluminum about one inch long and one-half inch high. There were 37 on each wing. Their function was to smooth out the air flow. The addition of 74 globs of metal certainly didn't enhance the beauty of the airplane but they did the job.

Tragically, Jim Verdin, who had become a Douglas test pilot after leaving the Navy, was killed while performing a transonic wing drop test in the Skyhawk. Jim had held the three-kilometer speed record in the Skyray. He was in an A4D-1 on January 13, 1955, operating out of Douglas' test facility at Edwards Air Force Base. At approximately 2:30 p.m., a Douglas dispatcher heard a brief, garbled, radio transmission and initiated a check-in procedure with all of our airborne aircraft. Jim was in a plane identified by Bureau No. (137815). Number 815 did not respond to numerous calls, and the appropriate authorities were notified of a possible downed aircraft. Simultaneously, a pall of black smoke became visible east of the Rogers dry lake bed. All airborne Douglas test aircraft were sent to the area to look for a parachute, either in the air, since the flight was scheduled for high altitude, or on the ground. Jim was wearing a khaki flight suit and a khaki parachute pack with an all white canopy.

It was confirmed that the smoke was caused by 815 and that Jim was not in the immediate vicinity of the wreckage. The terrain was relatively level with hills nearby rising to several thousand feet above the desert floor. Snow covered the upper half of the hills and made the search difficult, especially considering the white parachute canopy.

Jim's aircraft had impacted at a very steep angle. It was hard to decide from the air if he had ejected or not. An immediate ground search was necessary with Douglas' Flight Operations Department at Edwards assigned a radio frequency to organize and control the effort.

The search was limited by the early sunset in January but was continued until dark using Douglas test and logistic aircraft and other volunteers from Edwards. After darkness, I was one of the observers in the company's DC-3 which searched the area until after midnight, looking for a flashing light, bon fire, or any signal for help. We were very concerned about the cold temperature in the desert at night, especially if Jim were injured. Sadly, we saw nothing on the desert floor.

We drew a grid system chart of the area and delivered copies to various organizations and flight crews. The Edwards Test Pilot School and Base Operations, along with Lockheed, Northrop, North American, and some others volunteered aircraft.

At daybreak we launched a massive coordinated search, by ground and by air, including all the company's Navions. Since we could not determine where or whether an ejection had occurred, we assumed a ten mile radius from the impact point as an ejection envelope and to that added the drift of a parachute from 35,000 feet to the desert floor, based on the upper air wind data.

The huge team commenced the search and after a time, a ground party at the site of the wreckage determined that Jim had, in fact, ejected from the aircraft. Hope of finding him alive was fast diminishing.

It wasn't until twenty-four hours after the initial "aircraft missing" call, that Jim's body was discovered. It was partially covered by sage brush about half a mile from the wreckage. His parachute had not opened and subsequent investigation determined that his helmet was crushed by the canopy during the ejection sequence. Jim was probably knocked unconscious, or worse, and was unable to pull the ripcord on his parachute.

I was assigned to the accident investigating team. The reason Jim's voice transmission was garbled when he attempted to inform flight operations of his dilemma was because he had vomited in his oxygen mask. For that to happen to a veteran combat pilot, who was known to be extremely "cool" during his speed record run, the gyrations and uncontrollability of the airplane must have been more than words can describe. The flight recorder was demolished in the crash, but from the meager scraps of the oscillograph paper which were salvaged from the wreckage, we concluded that the single hydraulic power source on the aileron system had failed. While on the manual back-up system, the aileron fluttered at twelve and one-half cps with a peak amplitude of fifteen degrees.

As pieced together from the charred data, the sequence was as follows: the usual and anticipated wing drop occurred, followed by a loss of hydraulic power with its resultant flutter on manual flight control. In an attempt to pick up the wing with opposite rudder using dihedral effect (roll with yaw), the roll was aggravated. This occurred because the fuel flowed into the tank in the wing that was down, thus causing a wing heaviness that couldn't be corrected.

Bank angle increased, the nose dropped, and shortly thereafter, the airplane was out of control. There was no chase plane for Jim because the flight was classified as an "insignificant" test – one that had been performed many times before.

In an effort to further verify why the pilot could not recover from the slight dive attitude, the circumstances were duplicated in the flight control simulator. With the stick extended for manual control assistance, the total amplitude at the top of the stick ranged nearly from the canopy rail on one side to the rail on the other, at a frequency of twelve and one-half cps. My job was to see if I could recover the airplane. I said, "I'm not about to grab that stick because it might break my arm." It was moving that forcefully and rapidly, back and forth. It was decided to install a tandem-powered aileron system on the next model to provide redundancy in the event of flight control hydraulic failure.

A significant number of my close friends have "bought the farm" while flying in the war and while flight testing, and yes, while even flying in general aviation type airplanes. None, however, affected me as much as Verdin's accident. I felt *indirectly* responsible for his death.

Shortly after his speed run while still in the Navy, he was offered a test pilot job at both Douglas and North American. He confided with me that he was about to accept the North American job because they offered a higher salary and he wanted my advice.

I told him, "North American test pilots are dropping out of the sky like flies in the F-86, F-100, FJ and AJ. Douglas has lost only one pilot since the beginning of the war. Besides longevity, you want to think of opportunity. North American is only building fighters and attack aircraft, whereas Douglas is turning out the whole gamut. It's the General Motors of aviation, the reason I joined the company. Forget about the small difference in salary. Douglas has a much better risk bonus plan. You know beforehand what you're going to get whereas with other companies it's left up to the discretion of someone else at the end of the year."

Jim listened to me and joined Douglas. A year later he was dead.

Landing the Skyhawk in a cross wind was another problem to be mastered. On roll-out the upwind brake could not be applied to maintain directional control or to decelerate without the risk of blowing the upwind tire. This took place because the Skyhawk did not weathercock into the wind, that is, track into the wind.

The upwind wing retained considerable lift while the downwind wing lost its lift. As a result the airplane tracked away from the wind, that is, downwind. Adding to the problem were the long landing gear struts which were soft, and the small distance, or spread, between the main gear wheels. I had the sense the aircraft was going to roll over onto the ground. We tried many modifications to the strut pressure and the orifice size without success. It was only by developing a special pilot technique that the tires were saved and embarrassment avoided.

This technique consisted of landing on the upwind side of the runway, immediately slamming the lateral control fully into the wind on touchdown to attempt to hold the upwind wing down, while there was still some effectiveness, and then braking the airplane to a stop as quickly as possible, being careful not to lock the wheels. Keep in mind, this was a simple, lightweight, military airplane and did not include the niceties of a commercial transport which has anti-lock brakes and nose wheel steering, or in the case of a high speed fighter, a drag chute to assist stopping.

Wing spoilers were eventually installed on a later version of the Skyhawk, the A-4F. They were armed by the pilot and actuated by a switch on the main landing gear strut. The "squat" switch is activated when the plane is on the ground and the landing gear strut is compressed. Nose wheel steering was also installed at the time. The spoilers removed the lift on the upwind wing and nose wheel steering provided directional control upon loss of rudder effectiveness.

The Navy liked the airplane from the beginning. I checked out Lieutenant Commander Wally Shirra and Lieutenant Alan Bean in the Skyhawk when they came out to the desert to evaluate the airplane. Wally became one of the original seven astronauts and was the only one who flew all three space vehicles at the time – Mercury, Gemini and Apollo (in which he made the first flight). Alan made the first flight in the Apollo Space Lab.

Contrary as it may sound, in light of the test version discrepancies, the Skyhawk was a great flying machine when all improvements were incor-

140

porated. It not only served the fleet well, especially in the Southeast Asia conflict, it was flown with graceful majesty by the Navy's Flight Demonstration Squadron, The Blue Angels, for 13 years. The Skyhawk did, in fact, have these sound features:

1. Light positive static stability: Meaning that the airplane will fly by itself "hands off" if trimmed properly and requires little trim change with adjustment in airspeed.

2. Control stick centering: Allows the stick to return by itself to the neutral position when terminating a maneuver.

3. Low control stick breakout forces: Allows the pilot to make small precise inputs without over-controlling the stick.

4. Good response and effectiveness of the flight controls at high and low speeds.

5. High thrust-to-weight ratio: The higher the better for a military airplane to have a tactical advantage.

6. High engine acceleration: Allows immediate response of the airplane to accelerate in airspeed in the event of a go-around or wave off, or to gain a tactical advantage.

7. Excellent visibility: Particularly critical for fighters and light attack planes to protect themselves and important for all airplanes for the approach to landing – and to prevent mid-air collisions.

8. Central force position harmonization (force and amount of deflection for the ailerons, elevator and rudder are in harmony with one another).

9. Linear force gradients (the pilot force to the control stick is an increasing straight line).

10. Low trim changes (allows the pilot to fly the airplane instead of constantly re-trimming when changing airspeed or actuating landing gear, flaps,or speed brakes).

One item on the plane was not corrected. When beginning an accelerated stall, an abrupt roll of approximately thirty degrees in either direction would occur because of the asymmetric opening of the slats. Douglas had a solution for this: a cable tie between the slats (which were small airfoils that extended into the airstream from the wings at slow speeds), but the Navy wouldn't approve it. The Blue Angels, on the other hand, required precision control at all times, so they simply bolted the slats shut. Also, they were not flying in close formation when near an accelerated stall.

In retrospect, my work with the Skyhawk over forty years ago taught me many valuable lessons. The need for redundant, irreversible hydraulic flight controls for supersonic flight is mandatory in today's high performance aircraft. The cost of today's planes might even dictate a requirement for triple redundancy in selected, long range aircraft to provide fail-safe flight.

Second: There is a need for a mechanical, variable rate input device for flutter testing. If flutter analysis indicates the damping ratio to be marginal, the test pilot can not be expected to provide the proper input by a simple rap on the stick or a kick on the rudder.

Third: Throughout the design of any aircraft, continuous thought must focus on how the airplane will be used. Flight testing is normally performed in smooth air to obtain good data. Yet on the Skyhawk's first flight at high speed, under turbulent conditions, there was skin buckling, tears, and a missing piece of rudder.

Cross wind landings are generally not a problem when flying at Muroc Dry Lake or on the wide runways of Edwards AFB or NAS Patuxent River, but that's not the case for units operating out of single, narrow strips, which may be all that's available under combat conditions.

The fourth basic lesson has to do with spins. There is always some configuration that has not been flight-tested. A corollary is that small changes in moments of inertia can create large changes in moments of anxiety. Proceed with caution!

Fifth: Inverted spins need to be investigated early in the spin program, preferably immediately after the initial familiarization upright spin entries. Historically, it has been proven that an inadvertent inverted spin is most confusing, especially the first time a pilot experiences the sensation. Therefore, perform a controlled, intentional inverted spin early in the program, so that in the event an inadvertent one occurs, prior experience will help in coping with it.

The Skyhawk represented the culmination of my test pilot ambitions – the reason I wanted to get into flight test many years ago. The proof of the concept is that the airplane is still flying in the Navy's training command (two-place version) and was an "adversary" airplane for Navy pilots engaged in air-to-air combat instruction. Many are still flying in the foreign air forces of Kuwait, Argentina, New Zealand, Australia, Indonesia, Malaysia and Singapore. They are scheduled to be flying through the turn of the century. Flown by U.S. Navy and Marine Corps pilots, it performed admirably in the Vietnam conflict, by the Israelis in several of their wars, by the Argentines in the Falkland Island war with the British, and in the recent Gulf War by the Kuwaiti Air Force.

In April 1992, along with others from the Society of Experimental Test Pilots, I visited the Navy's Fighter Weapons School, Top Gun, at NAS Miramar, California and was surprised that Top Gun was still operating some A-4Fs. (The designation of the Skyhawk, along with all other military aircraft, changed in 1962 – the A4D became the A-4, with letter designations added to indicate the different versions.) I was also rather astonished when an instructor pilot said, "I would prefer to fly the A-4 in combat rather than the F-14 Tomcat."

Comparing the A-4F with the F/A-18 Hornet strike-fighter he said, "It would be a push. I like the smallness of the A-4, its nimbleness and its quick response," he added. Ed Heinemann would have loved to hear those words, as I did. It would have been fun to fly the F model because it had fifty-five percent more thrust than the models I flew.

Apparently, the powers to be were listening when I proclaimed at the first flight party that we needed more thrust. In retrospect, reliability of the Wright J-65 engine was impressive. I can only recall one problem with it and that involved a dead stick landing on the lake bed. It is a real pacifier to fly a prototype airframe with a proven engine, whereas if you have both prototype engine and airframe, as we did on the XF4D, the situation can become nightmarish.

I remember telling an instructor at Top Gun that I flew the Skyhawk before he was even born, adding that, "I wish there had been a Top Gun school in World War II. All the experience I had included twenty-five hours in the Spitfire plus firing fifty rounds at a tow target. Shortly after that it was determined we were combat ready and were sent to the front lines."

He was amazed at that, which is understandable because Top Gun students who are the top aviators in the various Navy and Marine Corps squadrons, spend six weeks in the classroom studying tactics then fly fifty to sixty hours practicing in the sky what they absorbed in ground study.

Ed Heinemann's Hot Rod could well become to light attack, close air support, and the various training roles, what the venerable DC-3 has become to the civilian transport industry. Many small airlines throughout the world are continuing to operate the "gooney bird" 56 years after its first flight.

The A-4's claims to fame included the following:

a. Its original design weight was only one-half of the specification requirement.

b. The maximum speed was 90 mph faster than the specifications requirement.

c. Longest use in a U.S. service for a combat airplane (with the exception of the B-52).

d. Used in many conflicts – Vietnam, several Israel/Arab wars, Falkland Island, and the Persian Gulf war.

e. Navy Blue Angels flew it for 14 years. Highest longevity of the eight types they have flown.

f. Was adversary plane for Navy Top Gun training.

g. Smallest jet combat airplane.

h. Safest fighter/attack airplane.

It also had an exceptionally good accident rate during its long test phase at Douglas. In addition to Verdin's accident, the only other A-4 lost with a company pilot at the controls was during ground launch catapult testing at Patuxent. The airplane was at maximum gross weight and it just settled into the Patuxent River.

The only production test airplane loss occurred during an acceptance flight by a navy pilot. He was evaluating the manual control system; it got away from him and he bailed out.

In summary, the XA4D was originally a simple lightweight airplane with a few problems which were ultimately corrected. The evolution of its development included sixteen different models and 2,960 aircraft manufactured over a twenty-five year production span.

One axiom says: If you build it simple, it will ultimately become complex. There never has been an airplane that did not get bigger, heavier, and more complex as time wore on. The A-4M version had the Pratt and Whitney J-52-P-408 with 11,200 pounds of thrust which was a 55 percent increase in thrust over the engine in the original prototype. Also, with the improvements in electronic warfare packages, new weapons delivery systems and increased external armament, the A-4M was a far better tactical machine even though it was bigger, heavier and more complex.

12

THE CADILLAC

In order to differentiate between the F4D Skyray and the F5D Skylancer, imagine the former as a manta ray and the latter, with its long fuselage, as a lance. The Skylancer was longer than its predecessor, by 8.5 feet, which increased the fineness ratio (the length divided by the width of the fuselage). More importantly, the extra length permitted the F5D to carry twice as much fuel as the Skyray (1,333 gallons, of which 449 gallons were in two fuel tanks in the fuselage). The Skylancer was a marked improvement over the Skyray and it's a shame the fighter never went into production. It was the best plane I ever flew. The Navy called the F4D "the Ford," and I called the F5D, a "Cadillac."

The newer plane's wing was 30 percent thinner than the Skyray, the key factor in reducing drag and permitting a higher maximum airspeed, but it was exactly the same in plan form. The Skylancer had a V-type windshield which also decreased drag. The center bar did not obstruct forward visibility because the pilot looked *around* the bar, focusing on objects in the distance.

The vertical fin was thinner, had 47 and one-half per cent more area and was 1.8 feet higher than the F4D. It had an extended tail cone beyond the inboard elevons and rudder. As to controls, the main changes from its predecessor were its pitch trimmers which could also be used as elevons. There were also four retractable rocket launchers mounted internally in the underside of the fuselage, a forerunner arrangement of the missile configuration for the YF-22 and YF-23 prototype aircraft of the early 1990s.

The tail wheel snubber was like that in the F4D. It extended in flight, with the gear down, to absorb landing loads; however, the main gear tread was 2.4 feet wider.

A splitter vane was attached to the fuselage to bleed off the boundary layer air near the air inlet ducts for the engine.

Empty weight was only 1,527 pounds more than the Skyray. The gross weight in the fighter configuration was 27,251 pounds when carrying seventy-two two-inch rockets, or four twenty millimeter guns with a total of 470 rounds of ammunition or two Sparrow II missiles. This increased the airplane wing loading to 50 pounds per square foot (the F4D was thirty-six pounds per square foot). The airplane was designed for 7.0 Gs at 20,000 pounds.

The primary commonality between the aircraft was the engine. Both were powered by the Pratt and Whitney J-57-P-8 with military thrust of 10,200 pounds and 16,000 pounds of thrust with afterburner.

I followed this airplane very closely during its construction phase because of my intense interest. At the El Segundo plant there were fifty to sixty people working on one aircraft at the same time. How they were able to do their jobs without getting into each other's way was a mystery to me.

The aircraft was trucked to Edwards for the first flight. John Brizendine was the Test Project Coordinator and a very capable man for the job. He was also an aerodynamics flight test engineer on the F4D. He rose rapidly in the company, becoming President of the Douglas Aircraft Division in Long Beach (of the McDonnell-Douglas Corporation) some time later.

Steve Tydeman was the aerodynamics flight test engineer on the F4D and the F5D, a superb individual. I could ask him any question and nine times out of ten he had an instant and accurate answer. If he didn't know the answer, he would hunt it down quickly. Jack Ridley played a similar roll for Chuck Yeager. It almost goes without saying that the link between flight test engineer and experimental test pilot is instrumental to timely success in the field.

While making the preliminary taxi runs up to lift-off speed I realized that the F4D brakes we had installed on the F5D were inadequate for the Skylancer's weight. This weight was about 3,500 pounds more in the interceptor configuration – and 7,400 pounds more in the fighter configuration, compared to the Skyray. The brake problem was corrected by changing to a new wheel and brake from a new vendor.

I was totally confident and genuinely relaxed before making the first flight in this great new bird. In fact, while sitting in the cockpit waiting for the chase pilot to check in on the radio, I actually dozed off and had to be awakened by the crew chief.

I took the Skylancer into the air for the first time on April 21, 1956 at Edwards AFB. The airplane performed nicely in all respects except for a very low amplitude lateral oscillation of a few degrees, approximately four seconds per cycle. We corrected this by "tightening" the looseness in the control system.

It took us a year and half to achieve supersonic flight with the XF4D using the J-35 and J-40 engines and a dozen different tail cones. We encountered all kinds of problems in the transonic speed region, especially tuck under, tail buffet and rudder buzz. In the F5D, on the other hand, proving that we learned from our mistakes, I flew supersonic on that very first flight. Reason: the aerodynamic improvements. These included the increased fineness ratio of the fuselage, which reduced drag; the extended tail cone, which reduced tail buffet; the thinner wing, which also reduced drag and tuck-under; the larger fin, which increased directional stability; and the powered rudder, which eliminated rudder buzz.

With the aerodynamic improvements, the trim change requirements due to tuck-under in the transonic region in the Skylancer were less than half. Although there was considerable improvement in this phenomena, the trim change compensator was still desirable to automatically correct for trim changes in the transonic flight region. This improved the Skylancer's qualifications as a "gun platform." The cost in weight for the compensator was only 24 pounds.

Chuck Yeager flew chase on me during one of my early flights in the Skylancer. As was his habit, he flew awfully tight formation. I was endeavoring to determine what was causing some low amplitude lateral oscillations, and he was so close to my plane that he could read the instruments in *my* cockpit. I didn't want him that near because I couldn't safely make any control inputs while investigating the lateral oscillations.

"You're too close," I transmitted. "I don't know what this plane might do and I don't want a mid-air collision. Please move it out."

Reluctantly, he backed off. In fairness to Yeager, he was a superb pilot but equally important, he had an insatiable interest in how other airplanes flew, what their characteristics were, how they behaved in the sky. This attribute certainly enhanced his reputation as a master test pilot.

The Skylancer also featured vastly improved stability and control characteristics in the power approach configuration at 113 knots. At the outset the Skyray, with its free floating rudder, and with the yaw damper *off*, had an average roll rate of only 7.5 degrees per second.

The expanded fin area on the F5D significantly improved the directional stability which reduced the reverse yaw due to roll, resulting in roll rates of 80 degrees per second in the power approach configuration.

Emergency manual flight control on the XF4D was considered unacceptable above 175 knots. Therefore, it was eliminated on the F5D. A wind-driven hydraulic pump was installed in the event of a malfunction of the normal engine driven hydraulic pump for the control system.

Perhaps the Skylancer's most remarkable improvement over its predecessor was its maximum level flight speed. The Skyray could achieve .9 Mach with military thrust alone, but with nearly a 60 percent increase in thrust using afterburner the Mach increase was only .1 due to the high drag of the wing and the drag caused by the deflected pitch trimmers.

On the F5D's initial flights we achieved a maximum Mach of only 1.39 because in this early configuration the leading inlet duct for the engine was blunt. Subsequently the inlet was modified with a "thinner lip" and this increased the Mach by .14. "Tweaking" the engine to get a slight increase in thrust resulted in a gain of .1 Mach for a maximum level flight Mach of 1.63 – a full 63 percent increase over the F4D with the same engine!

Of course, these changes to the lip made the engine susceptible to engine compressor stall in the high yaw or high angle of attack flight environment. Further flight testing was thus planned so we could go beyond the 62,000 feet and two G turns at 55,000 feet that had been attained. The splitter vane definitely was an asset toward preventing compressor stalls.

The Skyray had been designed as an interceptor of incoming subsonic bombers, so the limited maneuverability at supersonic speed of only 2.5 Gs was not considered disqualifying. On the other hand, for the Skylancer in the fighter configuration, improvement was mandatory. We achieved this by increasing elevon surface travel, increasing power in the hydraulic actuating cylinders, and hooking up the pitch trimmers to be used in conjunction with the elevons. We named these control surfaces the inboard and outboard elevons. With this arrangement the F5D could attain five Gs at supersonic speed – twice as much as with the Skyray!

Sometimes bad comes with the good and that was the case with the Skylancer. The lengthened fuselage resulted in reduced pitch damping. To improve target tracking capability, primarily in the transonic region, a pitch damper was added. This corrected the problem at an acceptable cost of 16 pounds in weight. A by-product of the pitch damper was the elimination of a mild pitch-up when opening the speed brakes.

The changes to the flight control systems, primarily the use of inboard elevons as a pitch and roll maneuvering control – instead of just pitch trim as on the F4D – caused proverse yaw in supersonic rolls. (Proverse yaw meaning the airplane yawed in the same direction it was rolling.)

We predicted high roll rates of about 420 degrees per second because the proverse yaw greatly increased rolling capability. I was concerned with the ability of the pilot to control the airplane when pulling Gs during high speed rolling pull-out structural tests. Also, the phenomena of inertia coupling, (combined with pitch, and yaw) was prominent among the century series fighters in that time period, causing the airplanes to go out of control.

The inboard elevons were modified so that they did not function as ailerons but as an elevator. This solved the problem.

Flight tests, in a limited flight envelope for inertia coupling, correlated well with previous design analysis. Therefore, we expected that this phenomena would not be inherent in the airplane.

There was a lag in pitch control which resulted in unacceptable longitudinal control sensitivity. Many changes, including the addition of a high load-feel spring, solved this dilemma, although the spring did result in higher stick forces of eight to ten pounds per G at supersonic speed, which was undesirable for a fighter plane.

The stall program for the F5D was very limited, which was unusual for a prototype military airplane. The reason, however, was because a delta wing design has a very flat lift coefficient curve at high angles of attack, with no discernible break in the curve. This made it difficult to determine when the airplane had reached a full stall.

When I approached a stall while in the clean (gear up) configuration, power at idle, I established a rate of decrease in speed of not more than one knot per second. I wanted to precisely ascertain at which point the nose-down pitch would take place. The Skylancer had excellent stall warning characteristics including general airframe buffet at 30 percent above the stall speed of 70 knots. I distinctly remember this number because of the unusual environment at the time: high alpha, high sink rate, moderate airframe buffet, low IAS, and full aft stick deflection. While researching for this book, many people questioned this low stall speed. As the old cliché goes: "That may not be the way it was, but that is the way I remember it."

Stall characteristics included a moderate yaw and a tendency to roll to the right before the spin so more tests were planned but not until a spin chute was installed on the aircraft. I did not consider the inadvertent spin tendency a detriment because of the F5D's excellent stall warning characteristics. Moreover, delta wing aircraft flying at a steep angle of attack with considerable power were in trouble to begin with. Reason: Full power is required just to maintain altitude near the stall. On top of this the engine is very susceptible to a compressor stall, which could damage the power plant or cause a flame-out.

I had hoped that the F5D, with its eight-foot longer fuselage and significantly greater fin area with a powered rudder, would permit a more conventional spin recovery technique. Unfortunately the spin program was never fulfilled because the F5D contract was canceled. Prospects were good however, that a conventional spin recovery technique could eventually be used. The conventional technique had succeeded in recovering in one-half turn from the inadvertent spin.

At any rate, in comparing the two fighters there was one parameter in which the F4D was superior to its successor. This was during sustained maneuvering, i.e. during a dog fight, which requires that engine thrust equal or exceed the induced drag caused by the imposed load factor. The Skyray was lighter than the Skylancer and had the same engine thrust, resulting in a higher thrust to weight ratio.

The Air Force's F-106 delta wing fighter was making its initial flight tests about this time, and it had the "coke bottle" fuselage (pinched in) that was supposed to do wonders in reducing drag. I asked Leo Devlin (Ed Heinemann's assistant chief engineer) why we didn't do this for the Skylancer. He replied, "The fuselage is as thin as we can possibly make it, and it doesn't make sense to add bulges to the fuselage to get the coke bottle effect."

The Navy Preliminary Evaluation took place in the spring of 1957 with one of the test pilots being Lieutenant (later Vice Admiral) Bill Lawrence, one of the Navy's most able flyers, Lieutenant Commander Alan Shephard, and Commander Gallagher, head of the NPE team. Three airplanes were flown in formation during the NPE, and a fourth aircraft was later added to the "fleet."

Gallagher proclaimed at the end of the evaluation that the Skylancer was ready for production except for certain mandatory changes which could have been incorporated. Alas, the program was canceled primarily due to lack of funds. This was unfortunate because the seventh plane was to receive the J-57-P-14 engine with 900 pounds more thrust. This would have increased Vmax an additional .1 Mach.

Douglas did subsequently propose a Mach 2.0 plus vehicle to the Navy, however, with the installation of a J-79 engine and variable engine inlet ducts. I was honored that Ed Heinemann chose me to accompany him to Washington DC when he made this proposal to the Secretary of the Navy and other high ranking Navy officers, but it was to no avail. The Navy just didn't have the money for two Mach 2.0 aircraft in their inventory. The other was the F8U Crusader built by Vought.

Thus ended the F5D Skylancer testing by Douglas. Ed Heinemann believed, as I did, that the airplane was a genuine winner, which increased our disappointment in never seeing it go into production.

The flight test program went so smoothly that there were only a few lessons learned:

1. All improvements are not exempt from causing discrepancies. For example:

a. The use of inboard elevons for increased longitudinal control power, when differentially deflected for roll, caused proverse yaw, which resulted in unacceptably high roll rates.

b. The lengthened fuselage for increased fineness ratio and additional fuel tanks resulted in increased pitch inertia and decreased static stability, and required a pitch damper.

c. The new high force feel-spring installed to reduce longitudinal sensitivity resulted in high control forces at supersonic speed.

2. Deep stall investigations require a spin chute. Even though 47.5 percent more fin area was added, the high angle of attack required to attain maximum coefficient of lift for a delta wing, and the flat characteristics of the curve at this point, caused the airplane to spin inadvertently.

3. The customer is not always right. The Navy should have authorized production of the F5D Skylancer.

Even though the F4D and F5D were radically designed supersonic fighters, and the F3D was Douglas' first jet fighter, they were the only military combat test airplanes which were not lost in crashes during testing by Douglas experimental pilots. However, one, an F4D, with yours truly at the controls, was badly wrinkled.

Eventually, the airplanes were turned over to NASA for use at NAS Moffett Field, near San Francisco, and at Edwards where they were used to test a variety of equipment, systems and airfoils. The Skylancer was flown on nearly 100 flights at Edwards to evaluate landing characteristics of the Air Force Dyna-Soar space vehicle because it closely matched the lift-drag ratio and wing loading parameters. I checked Neil Armstrong out in the airplane. He and Bill Dana, who were NACA test pilots at the time, performed most of the above tests.

The Skyray held five time-to-climb and two world speed records, the first time that a carrier-based plane ever scored such an achievement. The Skylancer was an outstanding aircraft in both performance and flying qualities yet it was relegated to the junkyard. Thanks to Bill Dana, one remains on display in Wapakoneta, Ohio, at former astronaut Neil Armstrong's Museum.

These years as a test pilot for Douglas were stimulating, to say the least. All told, I flew ten of eleven different models of attack and fighter aircraft bearing the Ed Heinemann imprint. I was fortunate to be able to test seven of them. They ranged from the SBD-6 Dauntless to the F5D Skylancer. Only two of these planes did not go into production. No wonder Ed was called, "Mr. Attack Aviation."

I have presented technical papers to the Society of Experimental Test Pilots on the development and demonstration of the AD, F4D, A4D and F5D. At the end of the F5D paper I quoted General MacArthur upon his retirement, "Old soldiers never die, they just fade away." I added, "Old test pilots never die either, they just write technical papers."

13

A WHALE AND OTHER TALES

I was involved in a minor way with the A3D Skywarrior, the Navy's largest carrier-based aircraft. I made only a few tests in it, but was fascinated by this Douglas product and intrigued by the fact that an airplane so big could be launched from and recovered on an aircraft carrier, not to mention its ability to fly in the transonic speed range.

The Skywarrior was Ed Heinemann's crowning achievement. Planners in the Navy Department in Washington told him that a heavy attack bomber which could carry a nuclear weapon could not be designed at less than 100,000 pounds. Heinemann brought the A3D in at a remarkable 68,000 pounds! It was driven by a pair of Pratt & Whitney J-57 engines attached to pods suspended from each wing. The wing span of the huge plane was seventy-two and one-half feet with thirty-six degree sweepback. The rudder stood twenty-three feet eleven inches off the ground. The top of the tail folded over so that the A-3 could be parked in a carrier hangar. Its service ceiling was 41,900 feet and it had a tactical radius of over 1,000 miles.

For longitudinal control in the transonic speed range, nose up and nose down attitudes could be achieved by actuating the electrically powered, horizontal stabilizer ever so slightly. The part that impressed me was the control wheel. It could be moved back and forth with low control forces but yielded no pitch control response at all. The big aircraft was totally unresponsive.

It was indeed eerie to sit in this huge bird, in relatively smooth flight in a slight dive, move the controls, and have nothing happen. The safest way to recover from transonic flight back to normal, level flight was to retard the throttles, which reduced the airspeed and the Mach number until subsonic speed was achieved. The swept, thick wing accounted for the ineffective elevator.

This was weird. My experience in the compressibility and transonic region at the time was limited to the AD, F3D, F-86, XF4D, XA4D, F-100 and the F-102. In the AD the limit Mach number was .75, and you could hardly move the elevator even with maximum effort on the part of the pilot. The F3D max Mach number was .845 and it was limited by buffet of the entire airframe. The F-86 in the transonic region was limited by an uncontrolled left wing heaviness. The XF4D had limited control for a fighter in the transonic region, but it was possible to maneuver the airplane in pitch. The same for the A4D.

Since there was no tactical reason to fly the Skywarrior in the transonic speed range, and a novice service pilot could very easily get himself in trouble, the service airplanes were limited to Mach .88 above 33,000 feet and .85 below this altitude.

The Air Force liked the Skywarrior as well, and its version, built by the Douglas Long Beach plant, became the B-66. It had a different cockpit, J-

71 engines, higher load factor, was heavier, and according to George Jansen, who made the first flight in both of them, the B-66 was not as good a machine as the A3D, but it did have ejection seats. The A3D had an escape chute for bailout.

Two Douglas test pilots and two flight test engineers lost their lives in the Skywarrior. Bill Davis was performing a high speed structural demonstration when the main spar of the horizontal stabilizer failed and he could not pull out of the dive. He tried everything to slow down so the crew could bail out: retarding throttle, lowering landing gear and opening the bomb bay doors. The men were apparently encased in their seats by the disabled airplane which caused enough G loads on their bodies to prevent them from moving to the escape chute.

Tom Kilgariff was conducting high speed, low altitude, yaw damper tests when the combination of his physical input to the rudder and the yaw damper signal exceeded the design limit of the fin, causing it to fail in flight.

Like the Skyknight, the Skywarrior had an escape chute instead of ejection seats. The Navy requested that Douglas determine what it would cost to have ejection seats "backfitted" in the A3D, but the results showed the price would be upwards of one million dollars per life saved. That was too much for the Navy budget, and the change was never made.

A Navy crew took off from Los Angeles International on a record-seeking, cross-country flight from Los Angeles to New York in the Skywarrior. They could not fully retract all of the landing gear after take-off because they exceeded the gear placard speed, and the air stream ripped off a landing gear door which caused a hydraulic failure. One main gear and the nose gear were hanging down in the airstream, but they could not get the other main gear to extend. They flew well out over the Mojave desert and bailed out, rather than crash land with only two gear down. The crew survived but, because of the excellent inherent stability of the Skywarrior, it remained airborne.

The Air Force didn't like the idea of an unmanned aircraft, fully loaded with fuel, flying over the desert near their base, so the Commanding General of Edwards ordered that the A3D be shot down.

A fighter was scrambled to do the job. The fighter pilot missed with his guns, however. This had to be the ultimate in embarrassing situations for him – unable to shoot down a big, unmanned, unarmed aircraft cruising along in level flight. A second fighter leapt into the sky. Its pilot also failed in his effort to "bag" the A3D. After approximately forty-five minutes flying on its own, the Skywarrior had lost altitude and with wings level, almost as if it were trying to land on its own, crashed into the desert floor.

A short time later, in March 1957, the airplane set a record on a round trip flight from Los Angeles to New York and back in nine hours, thirty minutes, and forty-five seconds. This included time on the ground for refueling. The same month, one raced from Burbank, California, to Miami, Florida, in three hours, thirty-nine minutes and twenty-four seconds. In June 1957, two A3Ds flew nonstop from a carrier in the Pacific Ocean to a flattop in the Atlantic Ocean, in a dramatic exhibition of the twin-engine jets' "long legs," or range capability.

In June 1952, during the Skywarrior testing, I was invited to Pancho Barnes' wedding. The Queen of the "Happy Bottom Riding Club" tied the knot with Mac McKendry, her fourth husband. To put it kindly, Pancho would never have been asked to pose for *Playboy* magazine. But she had a heart of gold – *if she liked you*. If not, you made her black list. Chuck Yeager's description of her in his autobiography was accurate. An even better account was rendered in her biography written by Grover Tate.

She used more four-letter words than any man I ever knew. She took great delight in shocking people, man or woman, especially upon first meeting them. Many felt she ran a house of ill repute. In all the time I went to the club for rest and relaxation, I was never propositioned by any of the female waitresses or employees. She had a sign over the bar which read, "We are not responsible for the bustling and hustling that may go on here. Lots of people bustle and some hustle, but that's their business and a very old one!"

At the same time, Pancho staged some of the wildest stag nights ever. I thought I was shock proof yet these exhibitions were astonishing to the point I kept one eye on the door, to make a fast exit should the sheriff and his deputies decide to raid the place.

Pancho's wedding was the damnedest affair I ever attended. It was the personification of a wild celebration like those from the days of King Arthur, or the Vikings. About 1,500 people showed up for the event which took place in a huge tent behind her dude ranch.

Pancho wore a beautiful, full length white gown highlighted by patterns of lace – -the first and only time I had seen her in a dress. Chuck Yeager was the best man and Major General Boyd, the base commander, gave away the bride. After the amenities of the receiving line were over, I distinctly remember Pancho announcing: "OK, everybody, help yourself to the food!"

It was as if she had fired the pistol to start a marathon. Everybody literally dove at the spread. Manners took a holiday. People were grabbing turkey legs and a bottle of booze and consuming them with great gusto.

Pancho excused herself and said, "I've just got to get out of this damn dress!" A few minutes later she emerged in her customary jeans, cowboy boots and plaid shirt.

I still have my Happy Bottom Riding Club membership card and carry it to this day with great pride. Pancho was an unforgettable personality, the great character of the desert, and it was a shame she was eventually driven out by the Air Force. The club burned down in November 1953, exactly ten years after I first visited the place. Ultimately, Pancho bought a small spread at Cantil, about 50 miles north, and started the Gypsy Springs Ranch. I visited her once and not a single customer was there. It did not succeed and sadly, she died of cancer, penniless and alone, some time later.

The irony of Pancho's relationship with the Air Force was that when General Branch commanded the base, she was honored at a "First Citizen of Edwards Day" luncheon at the officers club in 1964. Many old friends were there and afterwards, about 30 of us presented her a "portrait" of our hand prints in ink. After her death, Chuck Yeager acquired the hand prints. They gathered dust in his garage for many years. When Pancho's bar was dedicated in 1980 at the Edwards Officers Club, he turned them over to the Air Force. They are on prominent display there today.

During one of my demonstrations at Patuxent River, Commander George Watkins, a Navy test pilot, and I were at Al Shephard's riverside home one afternoon when we decided to go water skiing. There was a ski jump ramp installed offshore and since all of us were competitive by nature, we made a bet to see who could soar the farthest.

When it came George's turn, he asked the boat driver to go slower because he had not jumped before. He wanted to work up gradually. His second mistake was to lean back, causing the tail rudders of his water skis to sink deeper into the water. Unfortunately, they caught the lip of the submerged end of the ramp. He was tossed forward and slid up the ramp on his chest. George survived, but that terminated the competition. We spent the rest of the day picking wood splinters out of George's front side.

I met Neil Armstrong in the middle 1950s at Edwards during the founding of the Experimental Test Pilot's Society. Edwards, obviously, was a gathering ground for many of the early astronauts. In 1991 he was at the Chino Airport in California where Tony Cordo was painting my Navion. Armstrong was there filming a television project on the first flights of vintage aircraft.

"Do you know Bob Rahn," Tony asked Armstrong.

"Oh, sure," Armstrong said, "he taught me how to fly." I laugh at that, but am extremely flattered that Neil said it.

The Skywarrior went on to become one of the most successful airplanes in history. It flew in the Vietnam War as an in-flight refueling tanker and as an intelligence gathering plane. It also played an instrumental role in the Persian Gulf War of 1990 and 1991 and was a workhorse for nearly 40 years before being retired at ceremonies at NAS Key West, Florida on 27 September 1991. It was a magic moment for Ed Heinemann, the man who designed the machine that the experts once said couldn't be built. He was the guest of honor at the ceremony.

14

SETP

Some have described the period from the late 1940s through the 1950s as a golden age of aircraft development. We went from pistons to jets, so to speak, in a hurry. Despite the occasional hazards, I was proud to be a part of this transition as an experimental test pilot. We were in a fraternity of sorts. In order to formalize that "brotherhood," a small group of us, led by Ray Tenoff, an experimental test pilot with Northrop Aircraft, met in 1955 and began the process which led to the establishment of the Society of Experimental Test Pilots (SETP).

Our goal was to serve as an outlet for the exchange of information on problems experienced and techniques developed relative to newly encountered phenomena in jet test flying. We wanted to promote air safety, to maintain cognizance of new flight equipment and escape systems, to provide pertinent educational information to interested parties, and to broaden the professional relationship among the cadre of aviators involved in test work. We had no union-like inclination to arbitrate issues germane to our profession.

Ironically, our respective companies were cool to the idea at first. They feared we were forming a union for bargaining purposes, which couldn't have been further from the truth. Above all, we were very careful not to infringe upon the proprietary rights of any contractor.

Although the basic principles of flight, such as lift, drag, thrust and weight, never change, jet technology had introduced new phenomena – compressibility, supersonic flight, inertia coupling, for example – and much higher indicated airspeeds and altitudes as the flight envelope was expanded. Importantly, the fatality rate was very high for jet test pilots due to the technical frontiers we were entering and the inability to escape from disabled aircraft.

I was on the membership committee where we decided to limit membership to experimental test pilots rather than risk dilution of our focus in exchange for having a larger organization. We excluded production test pilots; service or endurance pilots who flew airplanes for lengthy periods to determine their reliability; maintenance pilots who made check flights after maintenance work had been done on aircraft; home-built aircraft pilots; chase pilots; and pilots of remotely-controlled aircraft. SETP was incorporated in April 12, 1956.

SETP's first Awards Banquet was held in October, 1957. It was memorable because an aerial event took place that day which cast a pallor over the proceedings. The Russians had launched Sputnik into space, the first successful satellite.

Before the banquet, in the hotel lobby, I was sitting next to USAF General Jimmy Doolittle, one of our first Honorary Fellows. He was noticeably distressed about Sputnik. He was with a number of older gentlemen whose conversation was mixed with expressions of surprise, consternation and disappointment. As for myself, I viewed it as a momentous event but didn't get too excited about it. After all, Sputnik was just a tiny satellite beeping its way around the earth.

It wasn't until 35 years later, when reading Doolittle's autobiography, that I discovered why he was so concerned. At that moment he was Chairman of the USAF Scientific Advisory Board, Chairman of the National Advisory Committee for Aeronautics, a member of the President's Foreign Intelligence Advisory Board, a member of the Defense Science Board, and a member of the President's Science Advisory Committee. America wasn't accustomed to taking a back seat to anyone when it came to such technological achievements.

There was a light moment at the affair when our speaker, Richard E. Horner, Assistant Secretary of the Air Force for Research and Development, mimicked a famous Winston Churchill phrase. He said, "Never under one roof has ever been assembled so much bonus money paid to so few." The pilots all groaned because one of our goals was to persuade aircraft company executives to join the Society as corporate members. Still, there was a round of laughter.

Fortunately, America accelerated and expanded its programs to overcome the Sputnik *deficit* and has been on the leading edge of space ever since.

By 1960 we realized that in order to grow we had to open up an Associate Member category to take on production test pilots who had at least two years experience in the field, and service pilots actively engaged in flying evaluation and performance tests, with one year of experience. We knew that a lot of our members came up through either one of these categories and that by joining the Society it would help him (or her) advance to a full member status.

The Society has continued to grow over the years. We have members in many foreign countries and a European section which sponsors a symposium in a different European country each year. In 1990 we had the first presentation in the United States of a technical paper by a Russian pilot, Valery Menitsky, MiG-29 test pilot.

The Douglas Aircraft Company, incidentally, has more Honorary Fellows in the Society than any other company. Eric Springer, who was Douglas' first test pilot, was the first, followed by Jake Moxness, who tested the DC-2 and DC-3 in the late 1930s, Benny Howard of racing fame, Bob Brush, Johnny Martin, who became Douglas' Chief Test Pilot, and Russ Thaw, who had performed a great deal of testing for the Curtiss-Wright company on the P-40 in the early 1940s, and later joined Douglas..

Our 13th annual gathering stands out in memory. The Apollo crew, which made the first landing on the moon, was given a special award by Bob Hoover, SETP President. Neil Armstrong, who I had checked out in the F5D, presented a technical discussion of his lunar landing and began by grinning widely and announcing with obvious relish, "This is the first time since I got back from the moon that I have had a chance to talk to guys who understand what I want to say."

Our one and only Honorary Fellow that night was Charles Lindbergh, the man who inspired me to become an aviator. I couldn't wait for the banquet to end so that I could go up on stage and shake his hand. When I did, I told him that he was my childhood idol and that it was he who got me interested in aviation. He seemed pleased.

A few years later, on a visit to Hawaii, I sought out Lindbergh's grave, which was located a few miles from Hana on the island of Maui. I asked several natives in the town for specific directions but to my surprise, most said they had never heard of the site. Finally, one man pointed toward a narrow dirt road, down which I drove, stopping often to solicit help. This led to an area near a small country church large enough to accommodate only a dozen graves.

Lindbergh's headstone was simple and unimposing. A border of small stones formed a perimeter around the grave. The hero of my youth, the man who had accomplished so much, had chosen a remote and tranquil site for his final resting place. Standing there, reflecting, it became very clear to me that Charles Lindbergh was, indeed, "The Lone Eagle."

The trip took an entire day, but I am very glad I made it. For me it was the right and proper thing to do. Homage to an aviator pioneer.

Currently, the Society has nearly 2,000 members from all over the world. Approximately 600 of these are actively flight testing. The corporate members have grown to a substantial sixty.

One highlight I'll always remember from the early days of SETP was the address Gill Robb Wilson, editor and publisher of **Flying** magazine, gave at the 1960 banquet. He included a poem which caught the panache of a test pilot's life.

> Ten thousand grand for a dozen Gs,
> And no one can take thirteen of these,
> And all I do for this princely dough
> is climb as high as the ship will go,
> And dive until the needle hits the pin
> In the gadget that shows how fast I've been.
> Then throw her in reverse control
> To see if I and the ship stay whole.
> If the wings stay on and the fittings tight,
> And the elevators function right,
> And the ailerons don't flutter away,
> Or pressures buckle where the pressures may,
> I climb again with like intent
> To prove that it wasn't an accident.
> Pick up Gs with a spinning fall
> To see if she's weak that way at all.
> I loop for balance and stall for glide
> And whipstall hard with flaps out wide.
> I spin wheels up and spin wheels out
> And spiral and slip and slam about
> In landings rough as the tank can stand
> To prove each step the designer planned.
> Then I taxi into an open ditch
> And don't get paid for the sonofabitch.

15

NEW HORIZONS

In 1958, after I had been in the F5D Skylancer program for two years, the Navy and Douglas formed a Weapons System Office which served as a single point of contact between the contractor and the Navy. It handled contracts, flight test data, engineering and manufacturing matters. I was offered the job as Senior Test Program Manager for the A4D, F4D, F5D and A3D, which were in various forms of development, test and production.

This would mean stepping down from the cockpit on a regular basis, a troubling notion. I had especially wanted to finish flight testing the F5D. I was working out of Edwards Air Force Base, a fascinating arena where quantum leaps in aviation technology were taking place, and I was a part of it. Most of the contractors had test hangers there and something new seemed to be going on each day.

At the NASA hangar, with all the X airplanes, the speed and altitude records were crumbling with regularity as aviation probed deeper into space.

Douglas had a stable of airplanes – fighters, light and heavy attack bombers, turboprops, and heavy cargo and jet transports. The company was a true "General Motors" of the air. At one time we had twenty-six test airplanes – more than the Air Force. In fact, the Air Force didn't always have enough chase aircraft to support the Douglas flight test schedule.

The job as an experimental test pilot was especially fulfilling in this historical period because I knew that I was doing something no one else had done before. I would land after a 15-minute test hop, and even if the test was a failure there was great satisfaction knowing that I was the individual who determined design improvement, and that the engineers would honor my judgment. Whereas, the poor guy who designed the system was probably worried for fear he might lose his job.

In addition, the Skylancer was a trouble-free program. I had had no "hairy" experiences with the bird. My luck, it seemed, might have come full circle. I mulled over the situation for a long time and concluded the new job held so much promise I simply could not turn it down. I couldn't fly test airplanes forever, so I chose a new fork in the road.

My office was about 30 feet away from Ed Heinemann's at the El Segundo plant. One of the benefits of the job – something I checked out thoroughly before accepting it – was that I would be able to shed my coat and tie and return to the flight line to fly production aircraft on a periodic basis. I wanted to keep abreast of the work being done on the airplanes, to be assured that improvements were just that and that they were being implemented in accordance with the test criteria. Fortunately for me, both the Navy and Douglas management were all for this.

One morning in 1961 I was in the flight office, dressed in flight gear, ready to sign out for one of the production A4D Skyhawks for a routine test flight. A young Navy lieutenant was at the operations desk. He handed me a form and said, "You've got to complete this questionnaire before you make your flight."

I examined the paper, which consisted of a series of basic questions about the airplane.

"Lieutenant," I said, "I've been flying the A4D for seven years. I made the first flight in it."

"You've got to answer the questions," he insisted.

"Listen," I went on, "I performed the original tests – even the spin tests – in this bird. I've got hundreds of hours in it."

"That's our new policy," he said, unimpressed, "no exceptions."

Standing there, furious, and a bit dumbfounded by the indifference displayed by this Navy lieutenant, a somber thought worked its way into my mind. It occurred to me I might have reached a milestone in my career. Here I was, a member the old guard all of a sudden facing the new.

"Well," I said disconsolately, holding back my anger, "I guess its time for me to quit this test flying business." I walked out of the flight operations office without looking back.

That incident signaled the end of my days as a pilot of high performance aircraft. Over a 20-year period I had logged thousands of hours in some of the greatest flying machines contrived by man. I had crashed four times, bailed out twice, had twice, inadvertently, imposed excessive structural loads on airplanes, gone through many other structural failures and survived countless other emergencies, including engine failures, dead-stick landings, fires, systems failures, and two predicaments from which I escaped by deploying spin chutes.

Over the twenty years of rather hazardous flying, the question comes to mind: Why did I survive, considering all the crashes and near misses? Fate? Luck? Who knows. It's a mystery. My CO in the 309th squadron once told me that in his service the thinking was, if you could survive the first 1,000 hours of flight time, the odds of safe flight increased substantially thereafter. Was I more deserving of some mystic attention than the next guy? There's no suitable answer to this question. It would be nice to have a solution, of course, because it could be applied to longevity.

Experience is probably the key. The more you fly, the more wary you become in the sky. Being wary, on a continuing basis, is a huge and necessary plus in any flying, but is especially applicable in experimental test work.

The Society of Experimental Test Pilots was founded to spread the experience of all fliers, to heighten interest in that phenomenon of wariness, to expand the exchange of unique knowledge derived from difficult and potentially dangerous test flying.

Another prerequisite for test flying is the very basic ingredient of self-confidence. The test pilot must believe in himself, above all else.

On the wonderful and memorably happy side, I had an abundance of golden moments. I preferred, therefore, to accentuate the positive and took the position that my life had entered a new phase.

My job as Senior Test Program Manger entailed ensuring that flight test schedules were met and contractual performance requirements achieved.

I chaired weekly meetings with Ed Heinemann and his staff to discuss aircraft evaluation reports and problem areas. This was absolutely essential if we were to keep the Navy's business.

Although I regretted not being able to complete the testing on the Skylancer, I got a kick out of having a part in all of the airplanes by turning over brand new ones to the young and eager Navy pilots who came to El Segundo to fly them back to their commands. They had a special look in their eyes, one that reflected their confidence in the product, and I took great satisfaction from that.

As it turned out, the Skylancer was the last new airplane to fly out of the El Segundo production line. In 1961, as a result of a cost reduction effort, the plant was closed, and the brilliant cast of engineers at El Segundo was transferred to Long Beach.

My next assignment was in St. Louis, Missouri where we worked on a flight test proposal for a new fighter being developed by McDonnell Aircraft, a company Douglas was contemplating joining in partnership. The plane was the F-4 Phantom II.

Subsequently I became the Test Program Manager at Long Beach, solely for the Skyhawk. Then, in 1962, after a year at Long Beach, I got anxious feet. I was 41 years old now, facing some sort of mid-life crisis, I suppose, and decided a change was in order. I asked my boss about reassignment to a new program and made a remark which has to be one of the most inane of my life: "One reason I want a change," I said, "is I don't believe the A4D has much of a future."

Some prognosticator I was. The Skyhawk had one of the longest production runs in aviation history – twenty-five years!

Anyway, I got my wish and was transferred to the International Military Sales Department at Douglas where we tried to peddle the Skyhawk to foreign countries. In the beginning this was fascinating work involving considerable international travel – Lebanon, Kuwait, Saudi Arabia, Israel, Europe.

I tried to convince prospective buyers in smaller countries that there was no need for supersonic speed in the light attack mission. Pilots would run out of their own airspace in a matter of minutes if they did fly supersonic. This was a hard sell because even though their geographic boundaries were limited, the countries still sought an attack plane that could go supersonic in level flight.

Eventually, I grew uncomfortable in the roll of an arms merchant, or more grossly, a gun-runner. One day we would try to sell the airplane to the Israelis, next day to the Saudis, then the Kuwaitis and the Lebanese. This was not unsavory to me, but it just didn't set well, even though business was business, and I was a part of it. I sought another change.

From international sales I moved to a space program project. Douglas was developing the S-IV booster for the Saturn V rocket at the Huntington Beach plant in California. It was to power the Apollo spacecraft into orbit, and I became a project engineer on the Man Rating program for the booster.

I flew the Apollo simulator at the Johnson Space Center in Houston. The simulator shook, rattled and roared with exciting reality during the launch phase. Later, I became Manager of Systems Integration on the S-IV. But the work was not exciting for the simple reason the S-IV was not an aircraft but rather a large fuel tank which accompanied Apollo for a brief six minutes during the launch phase.

When Douglas won the contract to build the Manned Orbital Laboratory (MOL) for the Air Force, I managed a transfer to that project, also located at Huntington Beach. At least human beings would be flying in that space laboratory.

Unfortunately, the assignment was short-lived because the space lab was canceled by the Air Force after a year. So I faced another fork in the road: stay in the manned spacecraft program, which was fascinating and educational, go back to the S-IV fuel tank project, or return to aircraft flight testing in some capacity or other.

I had been with Douglas for twenty-two years, loved the organization and definitely did not want to leave it. There followed a serious phase of self-evaluation, I reasoned that an individual must not only be "involved" in his or her work, but must like it, if any success is to be achieved. I wanted to stay in the manned spacecraft field, but didn't see a chance for that by returning to the S-IV Booster or the Douglas Aircraft Division. Thus, I arrived at the painful decision to leave Douglas, deeply regretting departure from a whole cadre of friends, especially those in the ground support crew.

It is not easy to describe what the ground support crew means to the test pilot. Whenever airborne I knew that each and every one of those engineers and mechanics was in the cockpit with me. They were as concerned as I was while performing maneuvers, some of which could be characterized as dangerous. The pre-flight briefings and post-flight debriefings were extensive and embodied the very "meat" of the test flight experience. I considered the engineers the experts, relied on them extensively and looked to them for answers. Heaven knows I questioned them continuously, almost every inch of the way, because it was important to know why they wanted this maneuver or that one.

Anyway, the bonds forged over the years with those men and my fellow test pilots at Douglas were strong indeed. It was terribly difficult to say good-bye.

I took a position at the Rockwell Company as a Research Pilot for the Apollo program in Downey, California. This meant *flying* the Apollo spacecraft, but only through the technology of state of the art simulators.

There were seven research pilots in the group. We performed all the maneuvers the astronauts were required to do, but never left the ground. We were involved in human engineering, trying to eliminate flaws which might impede the astronauts from performing their work in the relatively unknown environs of space. We reviewed mock-ups, made suggestions for changes and were in the Command Module (CM) during its production acceptance tests, checking out the systems just as a test pilot would in an aircraft. Each system was operated individually until all of the "bugs" were worked out. Then all systems were fired up using ground power to check the operation of each sub-system under mission conditions. We had to assure that all sub-systems worked together properly, to verify their electromagnetic compatibility, to ensure that all crew equipment functioned as advertised, and to check operation of specific alternate and back-up equipment.

Research pilots like myself were referred to as "in-house astronauts" while the genuine astronauts were called "out-house astronauts" – but only in the confines of the plant, and only facetiously.

The work was intriguing. It was like being an experimental test pilot all over again, except that the flying was in a simulator. And I was learning something every day, just as flying an aircraft.

I had flown eighty-seven different airplanes and never had to spend more than a couple days in the check out phase. During the war, a lot of aviators flew a fighter for the first time after hardly more than an abbreviated cockpit briefing on how to start the engine, etc. In the case of Apollo, my check out took a full month.

I got to know the original seven astronauts quite well in those days even though I had actually met most of them before at Edwards or Pax. In-house astronauts checked out the CM at Downey prior to its delivery to Cape Canaveral. After that, the astronauts assigned to that CM visited the plant and verified the systems by simulating the entire mission profile they were to fly, from launch to landing – a 24 hour, round-the-clock evolution lasting for several days.

One company research pilot *flew* in the CM with two astronauts during these full-fledged integrated systems test missions.

I was fortunate to be assigned to Neil Armstrong's Apollo Eleven, following it to Cape Canaveral, where it was placed on top of the "stack". Al Moyle, another North American pilot, helped check out its interface with the Saturn booster.

The Saturn rocket was 363 feet high, longer than a football field or a 36 story building. It was an eerie feeling walking across the open gang plank from the gantry to the CM hatch. I once told Wally Shirra, "I really respect you astronauts because it scared the shit out of me just being on top of the stack." Schirra said, "It scared the shit out of me, too!"

I was coming off the third shift one morning at 0800, tired, grumpy and not the least bit cheerful, as I hated this shift. I wanted to go home and go to bed, but was told that ABC television wanted to give me a screen test to determine if I was *qualified* to be an on-camera, technical advisor for the Apollo moon flights. I begged off, but to no avail. Jules Bergman, ABC's space correspondent, had to leave that day to return to New York, and they wanted the matter settled before he departed.

During the screen test I was asked to describe the Launch Escape System. My mind was not clear, and I made a snafu, saying something technically incorrect. "Ah shit," I blurted out, "I sure fucked that up!"

I figured that indiscretion closed the door on any television stardom. To my surprise, however, the TV people judged me suitable for the job.

For Apollo Eleven, the first flight to land on the moon, and Apollos Twelve and Thirteen, I was in ABC Television's New York studios, working closely with Jules Bergman. Jules was a first-rate guy who did his homework and had an excellent handle on the complexities and details of space technology.

One of my prized possessions is a detailed flight plan upon which I had written all the chit chat between Neil and Buzz Aldrin and the flight controllers. It started at 40,000 feet on the descent to the moon when Buzz was calling out the last 1,600 feet as a copilot would on an instrument approach. I was really sweating. Neil Armstrong was a friend of 13 years. And I didn't stop sweating until he said, "Houston, Tranquillity Base here, the Eagle has landed."

The "walk on the moon" was not scheduled for another ten hours, but how can you rest when anticipating a stroll on the moon? Indeed, the astronauts were permitted to do their thing three hours and 25 minutes ahead of the time line.

At 109 hours, 24 minutes and 20 seconds after launch Neil stepped on the moon and uttered the famous words: "That's one small step for man, one giant leap for mankind."

Months of preparation preceded launches from earth but on the lunar surface, the astronauts completed their own preflight checks in a couple of hours before lift-off for the trip home.

On Apollo Thirteen, there was an explosion in the Service Module resulting in a serious but manageable emergency. The astronauts had to use oxygen from the LM and circumnavigate the moon before they could maneuver for reentry into the earth's atmosphere.

Jules Bergman broke the news to the world but got carried away. With great excitement he informed the global audience that the astronauts were lost in space.

"Whoa, Jules," I said nonchalantly. "No sweat. The astronauts have oxygen from the Lunar Module, and we know where they are. They're not lost. We're in constant communication with them. We're working out the procedures to get them back. Not to worry." Also, being a good company representative, I tried my best to convince him the CM would bring them home.

Jules was frustrated and unhappy with me. The reporter in him wanted an exclusive and that exclusive was to dramatically proclaim three astronauts lost in space. But I wouldn't let him do it. He tried his best to convince the public that a disaster was unfolding, but it wasn't and the astronauts returned safely. (Hollywood, by the way, produced a wonderful movie about that flight.)

SETP made Apollo 13's commander, Jim Lovell, a Fellow. His wife told me the night he was honored, that she was immensely relieved when she heard me say on TV that the crew was NOT lost in space. She did say she was compelled to verify this with NASA authorities on the Flight Support Team.

Every now and then when I gaze up at a full moon, I feel gratified that I knew every one of the men who walked on the lunar surface.

During the Apollo program, Rockwell saw a need for the astronauts to travel on the moon to enhance their exploration efforts and the Lunar Scooter was thus born. Because it had to be transported to the moon either inside or attached to the LM, it had to be simple and light weight. I joined the flight test business to make airplanes light and simple, and that goal was best achieved with the Skyhawk. But the prototype Lunar Scooter was the ultimate in simplicity. It consisted of a small platform, not much larger than a man-hole cover, and waist-high, bicycle handle bars which the pilot gripped as he stood on the platform. Thrust was provided through a high pressure nitrogen nozzle attached to the bottom side of the platform and controlled by a motorcycle-type throttle on the handle bar.

The vehicle's attitude was controlled by kinesthetic motion: if the pilot wanted to go forward, he leaned forward; left or right motion was achieved by leaning left or right. Lean backward and he went in reverse. To terminate flight in any direction, he simply leaned in the opposite direction.

As the project pilot I was amused by the configuration of the proto-type. To me, operating the Lunar Scooter was like trying to balance myself on top of a bowling ball. The human control system was far too sensitive. With practice I could hover the vehicle, but upon translating in any direc-tion, the Scooter all too often crashed.

VTOL (vertical takeoff and landing) development aircraft programs entailed having the vehicle tethered. In our case, the pilot was tethered to a crane while the vehicle was allowed to "crash and burn." In reality, the Scooter suffered no damage because there was a cut-off switch to the nitro-gen bottle which functioned automatically when the hand throttle on the handle bars was released. We were only brave enough to fly the Scooter to the perilous altitude of five feet. Moreover, speeds did not exceed one mph.

Control sensitivity had to be reduced so the astronauts could avoid getting into "Jesus Christ" or PIO – pilot induced oscillation – maneuvers. Four long arms were added. These increased the moments of inertia and required more definite kinesthetic (leaning) movement by the pilot. Although this corrective action improved controllability of the Scooter, I never flew it untethered. I believed that I could have, however. A bit belatedly, I was prepared to follow my Mother's advice of 32 years earlier when she had cautioned me to fly "low and slow."

I also flew the Lunar Scooter wearing a fully pressurized astronaut pressure suit. We discovered it was actually easier to operate with the suit pressurized because my body was rigid wearing the outer garment. You had to make an effort to *lean* in the desired direction of flight.

We were unconcerned about stalls, stall warning, spins, high speed buffet, Mach effects, flutter, brakes, nose wheel shimmy, compressor stalls, or cockpit pressurization, etc. as we might have been with a conventional aircraft.

Several astronauts flew the Scooter, which turned out to be a fun experience – as long as the pilot was tethered. I distinctly remember one astronaut telling me, as we observed another flying the scooter, "We aren't going to travel all the way to the moon and then bust our ass flying this thing on the lunar surface." However, the Apollo program ended negating the need for the lunar scooter.

Apart from skills gained through intensive training, it was the cour-age of the astronauts and their talent in handling tight situations coolly that saw them through. I wondered about my own qualifications in this regard, and realized that certainly one reason I endured in the test flying profession was luck – a mysterious proclivity to avoid the swinging scythe of the grim reaper. Another was the natural, and certainly unearned, ability to stay calm under pressure. An incident entirely unrelated to aviation occurred about this time in my life, illustrating the point.

I was on a skiing trip with a group in 1968 at Mammoth Mountain in the High Sierras, north of Bishop, California. Eleven of us worked our way to the top of the mountain to take advantage of the previous night's precipitation which deposited a foot of fine powder snow on a treeless slope.

Clifford Scott and Bill Rosenberg were the best skiers among us and usually led us down an untouched slope.

I was not a good powder skier so got a quarter of the way down and stopped to rest. Scotty had gone the farthest and Rosy was about half-way down. The others were behind me.

Suddenly, a thunderous crack, not unlike a sonic boom caused by an airplane, sounded in the winter air. I looked up the mountain and was horrified to see an enormous white wave of snow cascading down toward me. Avalanche!

I was struck almost immediately by the leading edge of the wave. It knocked me down, carrying me along head first with the descending, churning mounds of snow. I am a good ocean body surfer and a fairly strong swimmer. Instinctively, I began to swim in the snow, executing the most vigorous butterfly stroke of my life to stay on top. With my skis and poles still attached, I knew if I were to survive I had to stay as near the surface of the white wave as possible, as long as possible.

I rode the crest frantically working my arms for several hundred yards before being stopped abruptly. The bulk of the wave had spent itself, but not before I was covered by at least three feet of snow.

I was scared to death but didn't panic. I couldn't breathe as the snow piled over me so I dug furiously in front of my face with my right hand to create a hole about a foot in diameter, trapping some air. Simultaneously, before the snow had completely settled, I managed to rotate my left arm upward, giving me another small channel of air space through which a sliver of daylight shone.

Fortuitously, I still had a grip on the ski pole with my left hand, and the pointed end of the pole with the webbed ring around the shaft poked above the surface after the snow had settled.

So, I had two sources of air, the pocket close to my face and the slender passage around my left arm. Otherwise, I was in a vise. Even though it had been fresh powder snow, I felt as though my body had been cast in cement. I could move my mouth, my eyeballs and twitch my nose, but otherwise was totally immobile. However, I was breathing for the moment, and that's all that mattered because I knew help would be on the way. Within a very short time I could hear the reassuring sound of voices.

Scotty had apparently tried to outrun the avalanche by skiing straight down the mountain without making any turns. I later learned that an avalanche can travel an incredible 200 mph. A human being has little chance racing directly away from one.

Rosy smartly skied off to the side, a sound procedure, and avoided the massive flow. Others in the group did the same. Some behind me were caught by the wave at the beginning of the avalanche but the snow only came up to their waists and they were able to dig themselves out.

The nine survivors began an immediate nose count, learned that Scotty and I were missing and swung into action. I was shouting most of the twenty or so minutes while submerged, but my voice did not travel beyond my snowy tomb. Then I heard an unforgettable sound: "Hey, there's a ski pole!" I had been found.

Had I been covered by six more inches of snow the tip of the ski pole would have been hidden from view and the story might have had a different ending. In a few minutes the rescuers had dug me out with their hands.

I was surprised that my skis were still with me and that my boots had not come loose from their bindings, and that the ski poles were still in my hands, especially that left one. It had spelled the difference between life and death.

I wasn't injured and suffered no other ill effects so joined the others to find Scotty.

We thought he might have made it safely and already gone down to the lodge to organize a search party so I skied down there, couldn't find him, then went back up the mountain with an organized search party equipped with ten-foot long bamboo probing poles. The poles enabled us to differentiate between the hard ground and a human body. Because we didn't realize at the time that Scotty had been well down the mountain, we searched the higher areas for him first. It took nearly four hours before we found him, down slope.

Tragically, Scotty was buried under six feet of snow and lost his life. It was a terrible irony that he almost beat the avalanche because the snow wave stopped no more than 15 feet beyond where he was trapped. Had I been a better powder skier and well down the mountain perhaps I, too, would have tried to outrun the avalanche with similar fatal results.

As the Apollo program faded away, I was assigned to write the proposal for the flight test of the Space Shuttle, with jet engines installed only for the initial approach and landing tests. This was a painstakingly complex endeavor and called for a progressive, step by step approach – more detailed than any prior airplane.

While awaiting the award of the Shuttle contract, I was transferred to North American Aircraft's plant, where the company had built thousands of P-51s, B-25s, F-86s, and F-100s and was now building the B-1 bomber for the Air Force. I became the Flight and Test Safety Manager for the entire plant.

Test safety was a whole new ball game for me. The University of Southern California had a year's course on the subject, but since I was the manager I didn't have the luxury of going to school for that long a period of time. I had to learn the hard way, by on the job training. The hard way included trying to install new procedures in people with a mind set which said, "But we've been doing it this way for years." Those words fell upon my ears at least 100 times. The job got done, but it was arduous, and a far cry from making a high-rate of climb in an F4D.

The year, 1974, brought a mix of good and bad. My father died at 79. Dad was a strong and successful man, especially in view of what he and my brother, Ivan, accomplished in establishing the Rahn Granite Surface Plate

Company. Ivan's deafness led to their hiring mostly handicapped employees.

The second bad event was my divorce from Jane after 26 years of marriage, a terrible experience for both of us.

But a good event eventually came about when I was transferred back to the Shuttle program in Downey as a safety engineer. I was delighted to be in the "manned" space program again. In Downey I met Feppy, my present wife, and my favorite copilot in the Navion, the airplane which has been a kind of avocation for many years.

When I first heard that NASA was considering "dropping" the Orbiter from a Boeing 747 in the air, I told associates at the plant, "That's the craziest thing I ever heard. It will never work!"

One of my assignments was to determine whether the Orbiter needed a drag chute to help decelerate the vehicle during the landing roll-out. The landings on the long dry lake bed didn't warrant the need for a drag chute nor did the long 15,000 foot runway at Edwards, with its excellent approach and roll-outs at the ends of the runways. Subsequent landings have proven that with everything working as advertised, the chute isn't required, as the astronauts have had plenty of runway left as a safety margin.

However, I was concerned with the emergency abort landing fields in Spain and Dakar, Senegal which only had 12,000 foot runways. These locations were to be used in the event of an emergency landing if a Return to Launch Site Landing (RTLS) could not be accomplished. Aircraft accident records have long shown that the majority of mishaps occur during take-off, approach and landing, and quite frequently it is not just one failure, but several which compound the situation.

The bottom line of my analysis was that for decades the Air Force had been using drag chutes on fighters and bombers as normal procedure. In these situations the pilot had the luxury of making a go around if he was too fast or too far down the runway. An Orbiter commander does not have the same luxury, and he is landing a winged rock as heavy as a DC-9 at speeds comparable to the X-15 rocket ship.

It wasn't hard for me to recommend the installation of a drag chute, but it fell on deaf ears as NASA is success oriented. It wasn't until eight years later that a drag chute was installed on the new Orbiter, Endeavor, which replaced Challenger, lost in the explosion.

Another major safety assessment involved the whole department. It entailed the need for an emergency escape system for the crew. We worked on it for months, the most thorough and perplexing analysis I ever experienced. We concluded that an escape capsule, wherein the whole nose section of the Orbiter is pulled away from the rest of the vehicle, would be very expensive and complex and could weigh as much as 30,000 pounds, thus reducing the Shuttle's capacity for carrying payloads.

Ejection seats were not very practical. They could have been designed for the four crewmen in the upper deck, but what about the poor souls in the lower deck?

The British had ejection seats for the pilot and copilot in their Vulcan delta wing bomber, but the remainder of the crew had to bail out the old fashioned way. This philosophy did not set well with the crew. Finally, we recommended a system that would "extract" the crewmen from the side hatch, a method only feasible in controlled, gliding flight.

Predicting the probability of the loss of an Orbiter was also a critical aspect of the program. I obtained all historical data from the major aircraft contractors in the US who had been involved in experimental test flying from 1945 to 1974. My survey included those contractors who were pushing the state of the art in fighters, high-speed attack, research vehicles, vertical take-off and landing, and high altitude reconnaissance aircraft. I purposely excluded subsonic bombers, cargo, trainer and commercial airplanes because I didn't consider them on the leading edge of this technology.

Using historical flight time data obtained just from North American, the catastrophic accident rate was greater than 100 per 100,000 flight hours. The summary of the inputs was an eye opener: ninety-eight aircraft lost or destroyed, sixty-three crewmen killed, forty-seven saved by bailing out and twelve surviving a crash. Over half of them were caused by the following:

a) Human factor - 11
b) Power plant/propeller failure - 11
c) Aircraft stability or stability augmentation systems - 9
d) Structural failure - 8
e) Flight control - 6
f) High angle of attack/spin - 6

We also obtained the accident rate for fighters from the Air Force and the Navy, which was less than 10 per 100,000 flight hours and the commercial airline accident rate is advertised at slightly less than one per 100,000 flight hours. My initial gut feeling was that with the large flight envelope of the Shuttle and the long duration of flights, the accident rate would equal that of conventional fighters.

I knew that no one would accept this analysis since the vehicle was designed with triple redundancy in most systems and quadruple redundancy in the reaction control system used for attitude control in space. I also knew that no one would argue that flying the Shuttle would ever be as safe as commercial airline flying, but that was our goal. So by simple arithmetic, multiplying the number of Shuttle flights planned per year by the number of hours per flight, I arrived at a total of slightly less than 100,000 hours of space flight in 10 years. The bottom line is that my study and methodology predicted a Shuttle loss within 10 years.

I gave the presentation to the Chief Engineer and his design experts. While no one in the room disagreed with my presentation, the Chief Engineer politely told me to lock it up and not give it to anyone, especially NASA since they were unalterably success oriented.

I am not proud of this fact, but my prognostication was correct as Challenger was lost in an explosion almost exactly 10 years from the date of my briefing and eight years from first flight of the Approach and Landing Tests (ALT).

By 1978 I was working on the ALT Approach and Landing Tests at Edwards. Ironically, my office was located in the exact same hangar we had used in 1943 when I first visited the base on the B-17 for glide bombing tests.

Except for some interior paneling, everything looked the same. In 35 years I had come full cycle.

I never tired of the amazing sight of the Orbiter sitting atop the Boeing 747 and was intrigued by the notion that when separation between the two took place during tests, the Orbiter actually released the 747 rather than the other way around. At separation the big transport dove down and away from the Shuttle in order to provide additional clearance for the 747's tail.

After ALT, I was transferred to the Marshall Space Center in Huntsville, Alabama to work on the Mated Ground Vibration Tests (MGVT). This program lasted for a year and was intriguing because of the enormity of the ground support equipment, which included the gargantuan cranes and tractors used to move the space ship. The crew was so proficient at this that the Orbiter served like a finely machined toy. The crew had transformed this activity into an art form, what with the small tolerances and precision movements necessary to lower the vehicle into the fully enclosed test stand.

When the MGVT program at Huntsville was completed I went job hunting and had a shot at becoming an "in-house" astronaut at Johnson Space Center in Houston, but the lure of California was too strong. I managed reassignment to the Ground and Flight Test Support at Downey. Happily for me, this proved to be another fascinating job. Our function was to act as back-up support to NASA/Johnson flight operations personnel. We had the identical instrumentation that the NASA/Johnson people had and the same communications capability. We could not communicate directly with the astronauts, although we could be patched into them if necessary.

If the flight crew encountered a problem and NASA couldn't solve it, we were available to help, manning our consoles around the clock as the mission continued. Rockwell engineers were more knowledgeable about the systems than anyone because they had designed it. Therefore, we would be able to save precious seconds when resolving an emergency by virtue of the instantly available expertise.

The one flight that I "sweated out" the most as a non-crewman was the first flight of the Shuttle Columbia, with John Young as mission commander and Bob Crippen as pilot. With Columbia, we had to go supersonic in the first minute of the first flight! In a big *cargo* airplane, no less.

The aircraft industry had developed interceptors to go Mach 3.0 plus, and one manned rocket ship (X-15) with stubby wings had gone to Mach 6.72 (over 4,500 mph) after being dropped from a B-52 over a long flight test program of eight years. Beyond that, a manned, winged, controllable vehicle was in virgin territory.

If lift-off and ascent into space was a nail-biter, I was drenching wet when Columbia re-entered the atmosphere for landing. The astronauts not only had the standard concerns of stability and control with a new vehicle, they had to contend with navigating to the Muroc dry lake bed. They were not plunking down in a vast ocean as was the case with Apollo.

Other major worries were heating of the spacecraft as it descended into the atmosphere – a new reusable material was being employed for the first time to provide heat protection. The approach was no big sweat because the techniques and procedures had been determined in the ALT in

1978. But the fact that the downwind altitude was 40,000 feet and the big cargo space ship (the size of a DC-9) glided like a rock, called for maximum skill to land on a runway, especially under "dead stick" conditions.

The tension was high during the communication black-out period which lasted an eternal five minutes. It occurred during the time of peak atmospheric heat transfer to the spacecraft. There was absolute quiet in the Rockwell Mission Support Room during this interlude and when the first radio sounds occurred – "Enterprise to Houston" – there were shouts of glee.

The Shuttle was an extraordinarily complex vehicle. I never did master that element of technology so critical to the shuttle's success – computers. They remain somewhat of a mystery to me.

I always tried to think of the Shuttle as just a big delta wing fighter with a huge drop tank helped by a couple of JATO (jet assisted take-off) bottles strapped to it for takeoff.

Obviously, Mach number has changed dramatically since the beginning of flight. Those vehicles powered by reciprocating engines are down "in the dust" when compared to those driven by jet engines. However, jet engine vehicles have leveled off somewhat in terms of Mach number. Yet, when you consider the Shuttle, which could be described as a cargo vehicle, it's astonishing to note that it can travel at Mach 25!

It's the same for altitude records. The piston/jet vehicles are well "down on the deck" when compared to the space cargo vehicle which can reach 170 miles. It could be said that time-to-climb records for the Shuttle are "out of this world!"

I was on the Shuttle program longer than any other project in my professional life – twelve years. It was great work and coupled with my "cockpit days," I feel fortunate to have spent virtually my whole life in aviation.

Also a singular highlight in my life occurred in 1974 while working with the Shuttle. That was meeting the charming and beautiful lady who became my wife, Feppy. She loved flying as much as I did, and ours has been a wonderful marriage during which we have logged a lot of flight time together over land and sea.

I did not want to retire until I was 65 years old, but there was an air rally for light airplanes that entailed flying from New York to Paris and I just had to get involved. So I stepped down from my profession at sixty-four and one-half years of age in 1984. Ahead lay a golden opportunity for adventure in my Navion, the airplane that Feppy helped me name, "My Shuttle."

16

FINAL BRIEF

I didn't win the New York to Paris competition, but it was a grand experience and the Navion held up well. Don, my brother, a retired Lieutenant Colonel and US Air Force pilot, was my copilot and while we missed the big prize, we did receive some equipment for the aircraft from many sponsors. I also was awarded $500 for being in first place at the end of the first leg, which became academic because I never received the money.

For more than 30 years the Navion has been almost a friend of the family. Feppy flies as co-pilot, and a wall-size chart in the family room in our Whittier, California home is stuck with colored pins depicting countries where each of us has traveled in our lifetimes, with or without the Navion. Feppy is still ahead of me in that department, but as long as the Navion holds up, I intend to catch up with her.

I have modified the aircraft countless times, trying to eke out another mile per hour here and there, hoping to increase performance while shedding weight, a la Ed Heinemann. The Navion, by the way, was a Dutch Kindelberger project when he headed North American Aviation – N-A-VION – in the 1940s.

On the way back from Tijuana, Mexico one afternoon, where I had had the Navion's interior reupholstered, four of us were in the plane and had leveled off at cruising altitude when there was a sound like a rifle shot in a closed room, accompanied by a rush of air. The canopy had come loose and lifted off the rails. Wind whooshed through the cockpit, a truly scary sensation. I grabbed the canopy handle to prevent it from flying off altogether, retarded the throttle to idle with my other hand and slowed the airplane. Had that canopy flown off and struck the vertical stabilizer, we would have been in very deep trouble. With the help of Scotty, the man who subsequently died in the avalanche and who was in the right seat that day, we got back on the ground safely.

Negative experiences like the above were far out-weighed by the positive aspects of the Navion, however. I have raced the plane many times, won my share of trophies, seen a good part of the world from its four-place cockpit – the Caribbean, Central America, South America, Canada, Europe, Alaska, and even flown over Abbyville, France where Herman Goering based his crack, yellow-nosed Me. 109 fighters during the big war. In a poor man's imitation of Charles Lindbergh, I soloed the Navion back across the Atlantic after the New York to Paris race. So, even though my test pilot days are well behind me, I still keep my hand in by flying this trusty old friend, "My Shuttle."

Looking back, I reflect on the airplanes that have been the predominant and indispensable tools of my professional life as an aviator.

The Spitfire was the best combat airplane for its time, the early years of World War II. It could take off in short distances from grass and dirt fields, climb quick and maneuver well. In the later stages of the war I would give the nod to the P-51 Mustang as the superior fighter, but the Spitfire was in a class by itself during the Battle of Britain and thereafter.

The Skyraider was a tried and true workhorse, capable of hauling great loads of bombs over long distances, and delivering them accurately. Plus it had the capability of carrying nuclear weapons. It just missed World War II but prevailed in combat in two succeeding conflicts, Korea and Vietnam, residing alongside its jet-propelled brothers as a reliable and productive member of the inventory.

The Skyknight may have been an old man's airplane, perfect for cross country flights, but it earned the distinction of being the first jet night fighter to shoot down an enemy plane at night (in the Korean War). It was a steady, dependable performer which did what was asked of it, plus a little more.

The Skyray was by far the most exciting plane I tested. With its unproved engine and delta wing it represented a new design concept. Being the first person to fly supersonic in a delta wing aircraft – and to spin it – were personal highlights. It had an extremely low stall speed, which often resulted in a spin, but the stall warning was outstanding. It was highly maneuverable at subsonic speed at high altitude.

The adverse yaw at approach speeds was excessive but was improved with the yaw damper. It could be entirely eliminated by the pilot coordinating his turn by applying appropriate rudder. The Skyray was the most intriguing bird I tested. Despite its deficiencies it was an excellent vehicle for its mission, which was to get to altitude fast and intercept incoming bombers.

The Skyhawk project gave me the most satisfaction. It was the ultimate answer to the quest for a lightweight, high performance aircraft. It was also interesting in that we literally threw away the stability and control specifications and kept an open mind on what was really required for the A4D. It was an easy plane to fly.

The Skylancer was the best airplane I ever flew and my favorite. It took to the air just five years after the first flight of its predecessor, the F4D. It was a fighter pilot's dream. It contained all the desirable performance requirements of short take-off, high rate of climb and service ceiling, good acceleration, superb maneuvering at high altitude, low stall speed, excellent stall warning and outstanding visibility. It had very good roll rates and vastly improved handling qualities in the transonic speed range. She had the potential of Mach Two Plus performance if the J-79 engine was installed. What a shame it never went into production.

People have asked how many flight hours I logged over the years, and when I tell them slightly over 10,000, they wonder why so few hours considering that I have fifty-eight years experience in aviation. Truth is, test flights on fighter type aircraft generally are of short duration, often less than an hour. Because we had to develop and analyze the data after each flight, it was not uncommon to fly only twice a week. You don't build up much flight time that way.

The quality of those hours, of course, was something else. They were often dense with activity and occasionally seasoned with real excitement.

174

Still, the greatest thrill of my professional life took place on the ground – on the flight deck of an aircraft carrier, as a matter of fact – rather than in the air. The scene was USS *Yorktown*, the World War II carrier museum in Charleston, South Carolina, part of the impressive Patriot's Point complex. On October 10th, 1987, I was among the first group of eight aviators inducted into the Navy's Test Pilot Hall of Honor.

This was a special moment because the event took place 30 years after I had quit experimental test work. It was very humbling for me to be associated with the other seven. The living inductees were: USMC Major General Marion Carl, Captain Robert M. Elder, and civilian pilot James L. Pearce. The deceased inductees were: Vice Admiral Frederick M. Trapnell, Lieutenant Commander James B. Taylor (for whom the Test Pilot Hall of Honor is named), Eugene Ely, the civilian flyer who made the very first US Navy shipboard takeoff and landings, and Commander Theodore G. Ellyson, the Navy's first Naval Aviator. That's some company of eagles.

At the ceremonial banquet that evening there were no speeches, but I asked for and received permission to say a few words. I told the story of the day I arrived at Patuxent River with the brand new Skyraider and was embarrassed because I didn't know what the term "wave-off" meant. Having started out as an Army Air Corps pilot and spent most of my life as a civilian test pilot – albeit flying Navy planes – I had never dared identify myself as a member of that exclusive fraternity known as Naval Aviators. I said, "Tonight, I believe I have finally arrived. I feel like I *am* a Navy pilot!"

That came straight from the heart.